IN THE TRENCHES

IN THE TRENCHES

answers from the expert to the toughest questions you face

Bob Ditter

American Camping Association®

American Camping Association
5000 State Road 67 North
Martinsville, IN 46151-7902
317/342-8456 American Camping Association Office
800/428-2267 American Camping Association Bookstore
317/342-2065 American Camping Association Fax
aca@aca-camps.org American Camping Association E-mail

Disclaimer

The purpose of this book is to provide an overview of issues with which camp directors should be familiar. It should be recognized that camp directors and others who run camp operations will require further education and experience in each of the areas covered herein. Neither the publisher nor the author of this book undertake to verify that individuals who use this book are trained appropriately. Nor do the publisher or author assume any responsibility or liability for any consequences of the use of information in this book. Further, the American Camping Association, Inc., and the author hereby expressly disclaim any responsibility, liability or duty to camp administrators, operators, personnel, any program participants or their families, for any such liability arising out of injury, illness, or loss to any person or organization, by the failure of such administrators or camp personnel to seek further training.

Library of Congress Cataloging-in-Publication Data

Ditter, Bob, 1950–
        In the trenches : answers from the expert to the toughest questions you
face / Bob Ditter.
                p.   cm.
        Includes index.
        ISBN 0-87603-154-8
        1. Camps—United States—Management.   2. Campers—United
States—Psychology.   3. Behavior Modification—United States.   4. Child
Abuse—United States.   5. Camp Counselors—United States.   I. Title.
        GV198.M35D58   1997
        796.54'068—dc21
                                                                    96-49401
                                                                        CIP

Dedication

I am grateful for the privilege I have had over the years to be taught by children —my patients, campers, and friends. I am also grateful to the many camping professionals who have supported and enriched my work over the years. In particular, I would like to thank June Gray at Camp Wawenock, who has been a spiritual cheerleader to me for fifteen years; Rob Hammond at Camp Laney and Marty Griffin at Camp Saddle Rock, who taught me to love and respect the humor, pride, and courage of people in the South; and Ann and Hobie Woods, whose enthusiasm and belief in camping is contagious. This book is dedicated to them and to the many camping professionals like them who are truly "in the trenches."

Table of Contents

unit five **child abuse and other sensitive issues** 145

x

The New Opportunity for Camping: A Deeper Commitment to People

Two bricklayers were working on a major building project many years ago. When a passerby asked what they were doing, the first bricklayer, speaking in a sarcastic tone, quipped, "What does it look like? I'm laying bricks." The second bricklayer thought for a moment and then said with a twinkle in her eye, "I'm building a cathedral."

The vision people have of their work has a direct effect on their level of commitment. This is just as true in camping as it is in other fields. A caretaker can think of him- or herself as simply watching over children or as helping to build their character. Counselors can be getting through a rainy afternoon or they can be contributing to the social and emotional growth of the custodians of the future. Directors can be providing a fun summer or they can be partners with parents in the year-round education of children.

When I first began working with camps in the early 1980s, I noticed that some of the most powerful aspects of the camp experience were unappreciated by a large number of the very people providing that experience. Too many directors seemed to be thinking of camp merely as a program of activities as opposed to *a formative experience.* Although camping professionals always have had an intuitive sense that camp was great for children, the actual benefits and the particular factors at camp that delivered those benefits were not often clearly understood and therefore not clearly articulated especially in a way that seemed relevant to parents. (I once had parents ask me, "Why should I spend over $2,000 for summer camp just so our kid can learn to ride a horse?" My answer was that their $2,000 was going to buy them a lot more than horseback riding, and that, if it didn't, they shouldn't send her. She ended up going.) Camp folks were in danger of becoming smug and insulated while being oblivious to the deeper and more subtle elements of camp. After all, what good is it to have this potent experience called "camp" if upwards of sixty million American children and their families do not know enough about its value and relevance to think about planning it into their year?

In the past several years, tremendous changes have taken place in the field of camping. Camping professionals, having become more aware of the complex issues that children *and counselors* bring to camp, have taken a fresh look at what they are doing. To be sure, there are many practices and core values that have successfully spanned generations of campers. For example, small group discussions and lessons on steward-ship of the Earth are as relevant and useful in today's camps as they were in 1948—maybe even more so. However, it has become clear to many that much of what worked in the 1960s will not work in the 1990s and beyond. Too many children and counselors come to camp with special needs—on special diets or psychotropic medications, with complicated disorders, on special educational plans—and under too many family, social, and emotional pressures for yesterday's approaches to be adequate.

Indeed, camping has gone through an evolution all its own. When it first came into being, camp was largely an extension of the school year. Children were taken into nature by their teachers so they could have an experience with their teachers and classmates in a different setting. These small bands of teachers and students developed into largely "Mom and Pop"-run operations that focused on community living and an appreciation of the outdoors. Indeed, Hedley Dimock and other camping advocates thought that merely being in the outdoors was ben-efit enough and that children exposed to this experience would absorb values and self-confidence almost as if by osmosis. Later, camps became activity focused, and skill development played an increasingly greater role in the camp experience. Technical activities like sailboarding, rock climbing, and mountain biking became more common. Camp operators built separate swimming and sailing docks, climbing towers, gymnastic and computer rooms, and ropes courses galore. However, some people in the camping movement were looking beyond activities, realizing that camp was contributing to the socialization of children through small-group interaction and interpersonal learning. Today, the most forward-thinking camps are sophisticated child-caring enterprises that, when well executed, are powerful participants in the growth and development of children. Camp, it turns out, can be a kind of vital and welcome "partnership with parents."

To be sure, camping is still fun, but, for the savvy director and a demand-ing public, it is fun with a design and purpose. In order for camp to be in a position to deliver the best-quality experience for children that it can, camping professionals must dedicate themselves to a deeper understanding of the social and emotional intelligence of all people, not just children. In its most highly evolved form, camp is well-planned and well-managed, yet it allows for the creation of spontaneous experiences that can make a tre-mendous difference in the lives of children and their families.

Camp, after all, is a contact sport. Camping professionals come into contact with a wide range of people in a child's community—teachers, parents, siblings, grandparents, mental health workers, religious leaders, and so on. Indeed, of all the camps that I have worked with, the more viable, dynamic, and (not surprisingly) profitable ones have understood that their success is in serving people, whether that be their staff (by giving them first-rate training), their leadership team (by developing its talents and tools throughout the year), the parents (who come to see camp not just as a summer pastime, but as a year-round and integral part of their children's education), or their campers (who are becoming more aware of themselves while learning how to be part of a community and developing greater self-confidence).

Leaders in these camps have instituted a number of practices that set them apart from their peers and have helped them bring their awareness of the more profound potential of camp into being. Some of these practices include

- Using a **team approach**—senior staff who design and deliver orientation, recruit campers, interview and hire staff, maintain contacts with parents, supervise staff, determine ongoing staff training needs and deliver that training, and follow up after the summer with parents, campers, and staff.
- Participating in year-round **staff development**—learning how to conduct more effective, efficient interviews; how to communicate cooperatively as a team; discovering which techniques work best in training staff; learning to practice active listening skills with parents, campers, and staff; and so on.
- Utilizing surveys and other **data collection methods**—finding out, from parents and campers separately, what programs are popular and why; what foods are desirable; which counselors are effective, warm, friendly, and helpful; what parents want for their kids; what help camps might provide parents in their role as caretakers; what children are looking for.
- Employing **experiential training techniques**—using activities and exercises to make training memorable as well as bringing in outside resources for staff orientation, training, and development.

In addition, many camping professionals have challenged themselves with informal self-improvement programs. These can have many elements, but I'll mention here a few elements commonly included.

Be a lifelong learner. Many children have told me that one situation they resent in any learning environment—whether it be camp, school, or home—is being the only one doing the learning. Because learning involves trial and error, and since making mistakes and trying new things reveal vulnerabilities in ourselves, the willingness of directors and staff to be learners alongside children is a powerful message to children. It suggests that everyone is willing to take healthy risks and be open to *looking at our own behavior* and *owning our own mistakes,* thus sharing in both the humility and the victory of being a learner.

More simply, it means that *everyone* at camp is willing to show his or her vulnerable as well as masterful side.

Challenge yourself to create a safe rather than just a comfortable environment for learning. By "safe" I mean an environment where it is acceptable to try new things without the risk of being shamed, humiliated, or ridiculed for being different or imperfect. We usually move out of our comfort zone when we stretch or challenge ourselves, just as children often do when they first come to camp. Indeed, in the first few days campers must adjust to many transitions—a new bed at a sleepover camp, new adults, new friends, and a new routine. The degree to which a camp provides an emotionally and physically safe environment is the same degree to which campers will actively participate in new learning, especially in social and emotional arenas.

Cultivate professional partnerships. Camps are laden with tradition, which can be reassuring to children and staff who look forward to returning to a predictable, dependable environment year after year. However, after years of practicing and seeing things one way, we can miss the opportunity to think about fresh approaches, to take a clear look at our preconceived notions, or to open ourselves to new ways of communicating and sharing ourselves. Cultivating colleagial relationships with other professionals can help in this endeavor.

First, working, reading, and sharing with other professionals, *especially those outside the field,* helps you stay abreast of new ideas even while engaging in an ongoing examination of practices at your own camp. Some of the most innovative ideas in any field come from adaptations of concepts or practices from other fields. Camp can benefit from being cross-fertilized by medicine, psychology, experiential education, manufacturing, sales, or a variety of other fields. Second, getting support, which includes opening ourselves up to the scrutiny and feedback of others, is important to the overall quality of camping. After all, taking responsibility for the safety and well-being of other people's children is one of the bravest and most anxiety-producing engagements we can enter into. Until recently, many camp directors bore the anxiety of this responsibility alone.

Make a commitment to people. This means being able to be *truly present with people,* whether they are campers, parents, family members, counselors, or support staff. While this may sound easy, it is profound and difficult. Most people allow the distractions in their lives to keep them from truly *being* with other people. When we are committed to people at camp, the effects are obvious and exciting.

Children love it when adults are truly present and "show up," by which I mean much more than being physically present. I mean being attentive to a child's interest, keeping promises, giving credit and encouragement, and entering into the "flow experience" of play or creation. If there is one major condition children in the United States suffer from, it is the lack of this kind of quality, adult involvement in their lives. Research clearly demonstrates that the presence of caring, appropriate, and attentive adults in a child's life inoculates that child against the many risks inherent in growing up.

For the camping professional who must juggle a tremendous number of details and relationships, the capacity to achieve the inner calm to be truly present with others is what makes a difference in working with parents, families, and staff. *It is a lifelong, personal commitment.*

Recently, the American Camping Association (ACA), which accredits more than two thousand children's summer camps, began to recognize the impact that camp can and does have in the lives of children and families. As a result, ACA launched a public awareness campaign designed to enlighten parents about the substantial educational, social, and emotional growth opportunities camp offers children. Its slogan, "Camp Gives Kids a World of Good," reflects this thinking.

Some camping professionals argue that they have known all along about the value of camp and that it is the public awareness campaign that is new. After visiting over 300 camps in the United States and having worked with thousands of camping people, my experience is that many camp directors cannot articulate in clear, specific yet simple terms what it is about the camp experience in particular that is so beneficial to a child's growth and development.

Camp experiences provide children with opportunities to develop what psychologist Daniel Goleman calls *emotional intelligence*—abilities such as good judgment and being able to motivate oneself, delay gratification, control impulses, or express one's feelings constructively. In his book, *Emotional Intelligence* (Bantam Books, 1995, p. 80), Goleman sees this set of proficiencies as "...a master aptitude, a capacity that profoundly affects all other abilities, either facilitating or interfering with them."

Most camping professionals have only a vague sense of this concept of emotional intelligence and are hard pressed to identify exactly what behavior constitutes social competency in youngsters, let alone describe how a child's participation at camp contributes to the development of either. Furthermore, even if some camping professionals are clear on both of these two points, the question remains: what good is it that people within the camping movement know about the tremendous difference a quality camp experience can make in the life of a child when only a fraction of American families take advantage of it? In other words, all of this value must be conveyed to parents in terms that make sense to them vis à vis their own concerns for their children. As some directors have noted, however, if ACA is going to crow to the public about the benefits of camp, camping professionals not only need to know what those benefits are and be prepared to articulate them clearly to parents and staff, they need to be ready to deliver them.

For years, child development specialists have referred to emotional intelligence as developing competencies in children—behaviors, skills, and abilities that are the foundation of sound personality development. (Activities that bring forth or reinforce these competencies actually *build assets* in children that inoculate them against disappointments, setbacks, and losses while strengthening their self-esteem.) This is where the true value of camping resides. It is an astute camp professional who can look at a canoeing lesson, the rehearsal of a camp play, or the conflict resolution session masquerading as a fireside chat and see the competencies that are being worked on. Suddenly, archery, tennis, swimming, rock climbing, group sings, and cabin cleanup are rich with subtle lessons and become the medium for transacting the crucial work of establishing these assets or competencies.

A list of these assets might include

- Learning to wait
- Learning to work with others
- Developing better impulse control
- Learning the art of give-and-take
- Developing perspective
- Learning to tolerate a greater level of frustration
- Being able to persevere
- Asking for help
- Recovering from setbacks more quickly
- Having a less inflated, more reasonable sense of self
- Learning to recognize one's own feelings
- Recognizing emotional reactions in others
- Developing acceptable and effective ways of expressing feelings (especially anger)
- Planning ahead
- Delaying gratification
- Balancing individual needs with those of the group or community
- Being able to assess risk

These are the building blocks of emotional intelligence, the enhancement and reinforcement of which goes on at camp all the time in hundreds of ways. Because camp is not school, where there is an emphasis on cognitive and academic learning, the contribution a camp experience makes to a child is naturally more concentrated in the social and affective domains of development. However, the camping movement will not approach its potential as a powerful positive influence in the lives of children until camps are uniformly safe, concerned about child growth and development, responsive to the concerns of parents, and aware of their own cultures and values.

Camping has evolved, incorporating the developing body of knowledge and awareness we as humans beings have of how we are as people.

Today, as never before, camping is in a position to be a pivotal player in the growth and development of children. To realize this potential, camping professionals must become more aware of the social and emotional needs of both children and parents. We must be clear, articulate, and specific about exactly how the camp experience makes a positive impact on children and then practice the profession in a more conscious, consistent, and deliberate way. *In the Trenches* is a resource designed to help camping professionals reach this higher goal.

unit one
camper behavior

Creating an Envelope of Safety

In order to work productively and successfully with children, it is essential that we first establish a safe environment. When children feel safe, not only are they able to join in as part of a group or community, but they also have the ability to lose themselves in play, virtually abandoning their worries and inhibitions to enter into a kind of flow experience. When children perceive their environment to be safe, they are more at ease about revealing their feelings, concerns, and the motives for their actions. When the environment does not feel safe and children are threatened, uncertain, or overwhelmed, they cannot make sense of their feelings, let alone express them clearly, and are consequently less able to learn or try new things.

It has been suggested that one of the main differences between growing up today and growing up thirty or forty years ago is that the sense of safety and well-being children once took for granted—that the world was basically a safe place and that people were generally to be trusted—is far less prevalent today. We do not have to look far to see evidence of the stress that may be eroding this sense of safety. With divorce holding steady at from 15–35 percent,[1] and violence climbing higher every day,[2] it is easy to see how so many children have lost a sense of emotional and physical safety in their everyday lives. Indeed, these are the stories of the children who populate camps today. They often come with their labels (ADHD, OCD, PTSD, BED, and so on), medications, special diets, and worried parents—all signs of the loss of safety and the presence of high stress.

The term "envelope of safety" refers to an environment that can hold children, provide for them, and be counted on to be predictable and nurturing. There are several key elements that make up a safe environment for children.

- **Trust**. An environment that is predictable, has consistency, can be counted on, and has simple and dependable routines is one that feels safe to children.
- **Encouragement**. Rather than being shame based, an emotionally safe environment encourages children to try their hardest, rewards success, and allows children to save face when they make mistakes.

---

1. The higher the economic bracket, the higher the divorce rate, which peaks out at 35 percent. The reason for this is that people who have less money simply cannot afford the lawyers and court costs or make ends meet by splitting their resources. Source: U.S. Census Bureau, 1990.

2. The National Education Association in Washington, D.C., estimates that a student is wounded every day in a school in the United States and that a child is killed in school by a classmate every other day.

- **Autonomy and boundaries**. An emotionally safe environment is one that recognizes children as individuals and respects the need for each child to have his or her own private mental life.
- **Clear and firm limits**. An adult saying "no" to aggressive or acting-up behavior is a relief to children, even if they complain about it. When children feel out of control, they feel less safe.
- **Positive models for the appropriate expression of feelings, especially anger**. An emotionally safe environment helps children express affect rather than suppress or repress it and reassures children that their anger, in particular, will not consume them or destroy others.

Obviously, it is crucial to create emotional and physical safety at camp, not only so that children can participate freely in their bunks or groups and have fun and learn in their activities, but also so that they can make greater gains in the development of their emotional intelligence. If children do not feel safe, they will not listen, open up, expose their theories, or venture to trust us with their true beliefs. It is clear that children learn best when they listen, but they do not listen unless they *feel heard*. The sense children have that they are heard is directly related to their sense that their environment is safe and that the adults in it are truly present and tuned in.

Children, in fact, more than anything else, fear three things that are directly related to adults being present and attentive—they fear being abandoned or rejected, being out of control, and being humiliated or shamed. An environment where these fears are present to any great degree is not one that is emotionally safe. Let's take a look at each one of these fears.

Being rejected, ostracized from the group, or left totally alone is a fear most people have. For children at camp it may be especially keen, given that they are away from their families (even at day camp). In addition, because they are in the company of other children whose impulse control they may not trust, they may not feel as safe at the beginning of camp as they might later on. Counselors need to be aware of the fact that children may not trust them immediately. Trust comes with time, which is sometimes frustrating for staff who may not understand that they must *earn* a child's trust.

The second thing that children fear is being out of control. Children, after all, do not have such good brakes. Once they get excited, they have a hard time stopping. If you have any doubts about this, watch a group of children in a friendly water balloon fight or wrestling match. What eventually happens is that it degenerates into a free-for-all that gets increasingly difficult to manage without someone getting hurt. This is why setting firm, clear limits can be a relief to children. Granted, there may be times when saying "no" is highly unpopular. On the other hand, who ever said that children always know what is in their best interest?

As uncomfortable as it often makes adults feel, saying "no" is an important way to reassure children about the integrity of the physical and emotional environment and its ability to contain their impulses even if they cannot do that themselves. When children become overstimulated—too silly, aggressive, frightened, or curious—they feel less safe, even though they may not readily admit it. (The safety of the physical environment is crucial in creating a sense of well-being, given that shoddy equipment, sharp objects, or poorly maintained playing areas convey lack of care and concern. Physical safety is an integral part of emotional safety.)

It is important to remember that children do not always have such well-developed internal control. Until children get better at controlling their feelings, they are often ruled by them. When they feel something—whether it is anger, jealousy, homesickness, or compassion—it is often without restraint. Unfortunately, their capacity to stop and think, delay gratification, and express their feelings in ways that are not impulsive may not yet be developed to a point where they even trust themselves and therefore feel safe with their own impulses. They often cannot apply their own brakes, and, when they do, it may be too late. They rely on adults for help with stopping, which can restore their sense of self-control and safety.

The most universal fear children have about their environment is the fear of being humiliated. Children even have their own phrases for this, such as, "I bet you *feel small!*" When working with children, it is important for you to be clear as to whether your disciplinary actions are designed to restore order and self-control or to make a child feel small. Barking orders at or humiliating a child does not create an environment of acceptance and emotional safety. It can destroy the trust that exists in the community.

Creating an envelope of safety, then, is about having an environment that is responsive to the true needs of children. When the envelope of safety exists, there is actually an alliance present with children based on an awareness of their implicit need for a safe environment. (We are "hearing" their need for it.) An environment that maintains clear boundaries, addresses the need for emotional and physical containment, and allows the appropriate expression of feelings, including anger, provides children with a venue where they can grow, thrive, and work on their emotional IQ. "In the Trenches" columns that address specific behavioral challenges, such as bullying, scapegoating, and teasing, illustrate a practical application of the envelope of safety. In other words, an empathetic understanding of and response to a child's behavior are based on a deeper listening, where the caretaker is aware of the need that children have for an environment that is physically and emotionally safe.

part one
general camper behavior

Today's Changing Camper

> 1. Children's more complicated lives of today require more training of camp staff.
> 2. Growth of ADHD and other disorders; girls on antidepressants.
> 3. The need to get information from parents on disorders at the start of camp.
> 4. The need to work with parents; they need help, encouragement, education.

Rob Hammond likes to tell how his predecessor, Coach Laney, founder of Camp Laney for Boys in Alabama, conducted staff training almost thirty years ago. "We would all get up to camp three days before opening day to get camp in shape for the summer. On Sunday, after breakfast, Coach would call us all onto the porch of the Lodge. He would remind us that campers were due within the hour, and that, during the summer we should '...remember to be friendly, firm, and fair.' That was the extent of staff training! What's more, it *worked!* Things have certainly changed!"

Indeed, things have changed. Rob himself conducts an intensive orientation that is typical of most camps in the 1990s. "I bring in two outside professionals just to talk about children. That's an indication of just how complicated life has become for youngsters today."

Jani Brokaw Williams of Campus Kids Summer Camp in Connecticut agrees. "It used to be that it was more the exception than the norm to encounter a child with special difficulties. With family life as unstable as it seems to be and greater awareness of drugs, violence, and family problems, aggressive behavior among campers seems to be the norm."

Rob's and Jani's comments mirror the observations of many directors and key staff. In the more than forty camps I visited during the summer of 1993, the experiences seemed remarkably similar.

"There are two things happening," begins Ira Seinfeld, head counselor at Camp Lokanda in New York. "People are identifying things like ADHD [attention deficit hyperactive disorder] in children in greater numbers before they come to camp, and the stigma associated with these conditions is dropping. Consequently, camps are seeing more and more of these children."

In camps I visited last summer, ADHD replaced bed-wetting as one of the top five challenges facing staff. Some of the other issues I heard about are as follows:

1. A greater number of children diagnosed with ADHD, on medication (usually Ritalin) or worse, taken off their meds just before camp starts
2. A greater number of girls, in particular, coming to camp on antidepressant medication
3. More intense rivalries and jealousies among early teen females
4. A greater incidence of aggressive and even violent behavior among campers
5. More parents who feel uncertain or defensive about their children

Let us look at the ADHD problem. Attention deficit disorder is thought to affect between 3 and 5 percent of the population in the United States. Boys are diagnosed with the disorder between three and four times more frequently than girls. Most camps are discovering that the stigma associated with ADHD is becoming like that of divorce in the 1960s and 1970s—at first it was something to be ashamed of; now it is something to get help for.

"Just four years ago, we would see perhaps one out of fifty with this problem. Now we are seeing maybe seven or eight," remarks Ira Seinfeld. "My problem is that I am still very slow on the uptake," he continues. "When we have a child struggling to adjust to life in the cabin, alienating his bunkmates in the process, it still takes me a week before I ask the child, 'Who is the doctor you see to talk about your feelings?' Then it all comes out!"

"Camp directors will continue to see these youngsters in increasing numbers," says Dr. Dennis O'Brien, a Boston-based child psychologist. "They are going to have to do what classroom teachers are doing—know what the disorder looks like so you can spot it early; become familiar with the medication issues so you can speak in an informed way with pediatricians and parents who may not know about camp; learn what behavior management techniques work for this group of children and teach them to your staff."

A crucial task is getting information from parents early enough so that the staff can work with the child and the cabin that she's in. Too often camps find out what the problem is after a week or more has gone by, by which time the child has already alienated her bunkmates and lost favor with her counselor. Many camps have instituted the use of a new parent information form that addresses ADHD and other problems.

Working with parents in the 1990s can be as much of a challenge as working with youngsters. "We find that parents need as much help and encouragement as the children," says Ann Woods of Roughing It Day Camp in California. "We do more educating with parents than ever before, especially working through challenges. Most parents want their child to be able to relax at camp. When that doesn't happen, they don't want to hear about challenges. Our job is to show them that camp is not school—we can deal with challenges here and most often get a successful outcome."

Jani Brokaw Williams echoes this sentiment. "There is more partnership in my work with parents. Once I learn how to address their unspoken fears, they are more honest and open with me. I finally realized that, when I called parents, they thought I was calling to kick their child out of camp. Now I say at the outset that is not what my call is about, and things progress past the defensive stage."

What about girls and antidepressants? "This is a disturbing development," says Dr. Sue Curtin of the Concord public schools who works with camping professionals on issues related to girls. "Many of the problems associated with depression have to do with girls and their self-esteem. Girls are at high risk for low self-esteem. Starting at about age ten, girls begin this downward spiral in their feelings about themselves."

So what can camps do about this problem? Dr. Curtin recommends several things. "The first thing is to educate yourself about girls' development. Then such things as developing a 'happiness list' and an 'adequacy list' can help some girls take stock of some of the positive things about themselves." More camps are also taking greater care to develop trust and a greater tolerance of individual differences at camp. Without this envelope of safety, young people do not open up, do not take healthy risks, and consequently do not thrive.

"If anything, camp directors have had to learn more about children and societal issues than ever before," says Jani Brokaw Williams. "Camp is a cross section of life—if it is out there, sooner or later camping professionals are going to see it in camp."

Dr. Curtin and Dr. O'Brien are two of the several professionals who discuss in practical ways the issues camping professionals are seeing in the 1990s. The need for this kind of learning is best articulated by Ann Woods. "Parents have high expectations of camp and we sure as heck better deliver. If we don't, parents will choose other options. When things don't go smoothly, we need strategies to deal with it. And camp is such a great place for children to master their challenges!"

8

Feeding Campers Hungry for Attention

1. Caretaking that provides a stronger sense of self.
2. Motivating children to achieve specific skills—ability to wait, thoughtfulness, etc.
3. Setting achievable goals.
4. "Secret signal" technique used by counselor with camper.

Dear Bob,

We encountered a challenging situation last summer from some of our younger female campers. Typically, an eight- or nine-year-old is tearful and sad during the first few days of camp to which our counselors respond wonderfully. Some of these campers, however, are forever seeking attention. They cling to counselors, cry about the smallest things, and just plum wear out our staff!

Can you give us some ideas about coping with these hungry children that will save our staff?

Beyond Homesick

Dear Beyond,

"Hungry" is an apt description for children who crave attention and affection from staff. This challenge, which can come from boys as well as girls, is especially vexing for counselors because of the strong feelings these children evoke. At first, their neediness stirs a desire to nurture and protect. After a few days, when it becomes apparent that no amount of attention seems to fill these children up, counselors begin to feel discouraged, overwhelmed, and frustrated.

To complicate the picture, many staff members come to resent the constant intrusion into their privacy these children seem to demand. Counselor resentment can increase the risk of counselors being mean to campers. It can also result in tremendous guilt because counselors feel they are being mean when they set limits with these children. All of these dynamics have a terrible negative impact on staff morale.

I suggest a comprehensive approach that includes giving staff

- **Understanding** of the issues
- **Strategy** or overall approach
- **Tools** for helping them achieve success

You can create a better understanding of needy children and show counselors how to respond to them more effectively by making a distinction between two basic types of caretaking. The distinction is between caretaking that provides *immediate gratification* and caretaking that contributes to a *stronger sense of self*. Attention-hungry children are often like youngsters who are looking for the quick, empty calories of sugar rather than the sustaining calories of complex carbohydrates or the body-building calories of protein. Sitting on a counselor's lap, showing off artwork, or winning the pride and approval of staff are the sweet things we all like to have happen at camp. However, children who want to make a constant and steady diet of this are like kids who want to live on ice cream and candy—it is great to have dessert, but we all need proper nourishment.

Children who want only immediate gratification and attention on demand suffer from a lingering internal hunger. It is as if these youngsters have a bottomless pit when it comes to attention—no amount ever seems to be enough. Such children have not developed a strong ego, by which I mean qualities like strong coping skills, resourcefulness, the capacity to delay gratification, belief in themselves, and so on. Staff would be missing a tremendous opportunity to perform a different order of caretaking if they did not make an attempt to build character.

The strategy I suggest for meeting this challenge is to use what these children want (for example, attention, interest, praise, affection) to motivate them to achieve certain specific goals (such as the ability to wait, thoughtfulness, and the need to help others). This strategy works only when the following conditions are present or carefully arranged.

1. The child in question clearly wants something from staff (affection, attention, time, and so on).
2. All the staff buy into the program and adhere to it (to prevent the child from playing one staff member against another and to prevent other staff members from unwittingly sabotaging the program).
3. One staff person (who has the best relationship with the child) coordinates the program.
4. Goals are set for the child. These goals need to be specific, simple, achievable, and stated in the positive. Start with only two or three. Examples include: ask before you show me something; ask permission before you lean on me, hold my hand, or sit on my lap; help out during cleanup/wake-up time without whining.
5. The program is reviewed and adjusted periodically.

Once the program has been spelled out clearly, counselors will need specific tools to carry it out. The first tool is some kind of secret signal, known only to the counselor and the child, that conveys praise. Best choices are things like a wink or thumbs-up. I always add a smile and sometimes a "way to go!" These reinforcers are best when they do not involve direct physical contact such as a pat on the back, since contact can be overstimulating for a child trying to develop better impulse control.

When a child forgets to do what is asked or slips up (regresses), a second useful tool is the phrase, "Oh, Erica! You almost forgot. Remember? You meant to ask me first." This is meant as a friendly prompt to get a child back on track.

If a child doesn't buy into the program, the counselor will need to be firm about sticking to the agreement with a reminder that the only way to get the big payoff (such as sitting on a counselor's lap—in full view of everyone else, of course—or getting to help with a special job) is to keep the agreements.

Another helpful tool is to use the phrase, "I like it better when you (do this or do that)." For example, Erica sits on the counselor's lap. The counselor says, "Erica, I like it better when you ask me first." Then follow up with the request, "Erica, I'd like you to ask me, now." Praise Erica when she does. Withdraw your lap when she does not.

Astute directors will find many uses for these tools, but they are more effective when used as part of a specific program and with a better understanding of needy children.

One further note: Many counselors are confused between setting firm limits and being mean. As I have already mentioned, children who have learned how to manipulate adults often evoke strong feelings of guilt in younger, less experienced or especially sympathetic staff. I would be sure to cover this issue—limits and firmness versus being mean—during staff training. You do not have to set limits in a condescending, sadistic, or hostile manner. Likewise, setting firm limits can help a child build character, whereas always giving children everything they want, while building counselor popularity (which is fickle at best), perpetuates dependency in campers.

11

Building a Child's Self-Esteem to the Stars

1. Low self-esteem keeps kids from participating and having fun; what builds self- esteem.
2. Unwittingly rewarding negative behavior.
3. Build self-esteem through action. A list of easy activities.
4. Calling parents about success, positive news.

Dear Bob,

We experienced a particularly frustrating situation with one of our campers that we were not able to make much progress with last summer. We had a youngster who seemed to feel especially inadequate and who shied away from trying any of the wonderful activities we have. He seemed to be a somewhat sheltered boy, though what made him so shy or unwilling to try things was not apparent to us.

Whenever a counselor would ask this boy why he didn't want to try, he had about the same answer, which was simply, "I can't." We realized that he needed a lot of encouragement, but trying to build him up seemed to have a limited impact.

What suggestions do you have for a camper who holds back in this way?

**Sincerely,
Concerned in Colorado**

Dear Concerned,

Children who feel inadequate and whose low self-esteem gets in the way of having fun and trying new activities can be especially frustrating for staff. One of the serious consequences of low self-esteem is the tendency for such children to avoid taking healthy risks, like trying a new swimming stroke or doing something on the adventure course. This in turn prevents them from growing and experiencing the successes that actually lead to increased self-esteem. In this way low self-esteem feeds on itself, creating a vicious cycle that can be extremely debilitating for a child or for staff trying to work with that child.

Trying to "talk up" such children—that is, trying to build up their confidence by convincing them they can do it—while making sense as a first line of action, may actually backfire in the case of an especially self-conscious youngster. If this strategy does not work within a short period of time, it may unwittingly reinforce the negative behavior by rewarding it through increased attention and one-on-one concern from

12

staff member to child. There can even be a manipulative aspect to children who need constant propping up, in that their inability to take risks or try new things results in a kind of secondary gain through all the attention they gain from staff. A staff member with a strong rescue fantasy—that is, visions of grandly saving children from their miseries—may become intertwined in a kind of dance with such a child in a way that is counterproductive.

My suggestion is to find some activities, special jobs, or other ways this child can both experience success, even in little ways, as well as feel like he or she is making a contribution. This strategy may take some creative thinking, but things like feeding animals at the nature hut, helping the arts and crafts instructor with supplies, raising the flag at colors, or handing out snacks can give a youngster some sense of being special in a way that is simultaneously helpful to camp. You must be careful to build on these successes and to not simply leave the child in the position of being perceived as the counselor's pet. You do this by moving from one such special activity to a more mainstream camp activity that all the youngsters participate in. Otherwise, you may unwittingly reinforce helplessness with special attention through the creation of these alternate activities.

It helps to keep in mind that the most effective way to build a child's self-esteem and sense of competence is through action—taking graduated, safe, supervised risks; accepting help; and not fending off friends for fear of being hurt or humiliated. The key is not accepting a child's helplessness, but finding these gradual ways of building in success. I like to remind staff that children are victims only when we allow them to be.

13

Helping Children Master Self-Control

1. Fear of losing control.
2. Empathy vs. permissiveness.
3. When to allow rule breaking (to build individuality) and when not.
4. Playing out impulses in safe ways.
5. Unresolved authority issues in staff.

Dear Bob,

Our staff has discussed children's need to break rules. We've had a lot of controversy about this. At one extreme, people allow children to break certain rules because it encourages individuality when children may be at a stage when they need to challenge authority. At the other extreme, letting kids break rules provides mixed messages about the need for rules. These rules wouldn't exist if it weren't important that they be followed.

It's tough to train staff to handle challenges from campers because the staff themselves are in a stage of challenging authority. They empathize with the kids.

Liz Ohle, Arizona

Dear Liz,

Thank you for verbalizing the dilemma of power, control, and authority in children, which is a fundamental one for directors and counselors.

Children fear two things more than anything: being humiliated and losing control. In responding to your letter, I want to focus on the fear that children have of losing control.

Fairy tales are filled with references to the fear of losing control. The big bad wolves and monsters we read about are actually inside us, a product of our collective imaginations, and they represent our most primitive and basal impulses. Children are compelled by such stories because they reflect the drama between impulse and control being played out inside them.

Civilization depends on the development of self-control, which is achieved through adherence to laws, rules, rituals, and sanctions in society. When children feel they are losing control, they become quite afraid. For children, losing control has such terrible consequences that they can barely speak of them.

Knowing this about children changes our definition of empathy. Many people confuse empathy with permissiveness, but they are profoundly distinct. Allowing children to break rules or permitting overstimulating situations can be confusing and even worrisome to children. It threatens their self-control, which they are still struggling to establish. To allow these things is to abandon children in their time of need, for, if they cannot control their own impulses, who will help them?

In other words, being there for kids is sometimes saying "no" or "stop." Counselors fear that saying "no" lets kids down (and threatens their own popularity or friendship with those children). The truth is that, when done in a nonpunitive, face-saving way, saying "no" can be extremely reassuring. Likewise, being clear and firm about the rules is truly empathetic because it responds to a child's deeper need for control. This should be included as part of what we mean when we talk about providing a safe environment for children.

I have often been in the company of children who must suffer the guilt and shame that accompanies the aftermath of having been out of control. By challenging us on rules such as wearing life vests while canoeing, children are really asking, "Can I count on you to help me be safe and put on the brakes *all* the time?"

I often coach counselors to say to children, "What kind of counselor—what kind of *friend*—would I be if I just let you run wild?" Children will often tease by answering, "You'd be a good friend!" Of course that's what they answer. Tell your staff it's for three reasons: it tests us; it tests *them*—there is often a daredevil quality to challenging authority; it reveals their inexperience—children don't always know what is in their best interest.

Camp is a rich place for children to practice self-control. In fact, I often tell children that growing up is really about mastering feelings and that camp is a great place to do it. Storytelling, puppet play, and certain counselor-camper competitions (e.g., "keep-away" played in the water) are great avenues for impulses to be played out in safe ways.

Pranks can also be a safe way to play out the challenge of authority, as long as there is no destruction of property or violation of another person's well-being and no one gets hurt. For instance, the girls at a girls' camp stole into the night and completely decorated the dining hall of a neighboring boys' camp, leaving only mysterious, nonoffensive notes at all the tables. It was a great hit. A word of caution is necessary, however. With young, inexperienced, or especially eager counselors, even pranks can get out of hand. A clear discussion with staff regarding guidelines and getting prior approval would minimize these dangers.

You can help staff deal with their own unresolved authority issues by pointing out that their job is not to allow children to break rules, but to allow children to save face when they goof up, to help them repair their mistakes, and to set more reasonable expectations for them. Children

15

are naturally dependent, imperfect, messy, noisy, immature, and vulnerable. It is their nature to break the rules. It is our job to respond by being clear, firm, nonpunitive, consistent, and fair.

Someone once suggested that a childhood society with no stops or limits would resemble *Lord of the Flies*—primitive, frightening, and unpredictable. Others say that *Lord of the Flies* is not so much about inner evil as it is about the failure of caring adults to impart a strong inner sense of self-control to children. After all, if our goal is for children to develop control that is internal, we must first provide them with a respect for authority and control that is external. A strong camp helps counselors help campers do that.

Encouraging Growth

1. Children say "I can't" without really trying.
2. Extinguishing "I can't!"
3. Magic phrases for campers to get your attention.

Dear Bob,

I am the director of riding at a girls' sleep-away camp in North Carolina. I am writing to you about a problem that often crops up with campers during riding lessons.

The other instructors and I have noticed that, when we have campers on horses in the ring learning some new techniques, they often respond to our directions with cries of "I can't do it! I can't!"

What is frustrating about this is that most of the time these campers are not even trying. I think they are just competing for attention and are not interested in the lesson itself. This response is more likely to come from younger campers or less experienced riders. Unfortunately, it is very difficult to conduct a decent lesson when campers react this way.

Do you have any suggestions about how to help the campers get off of such a negative way of reacting?

Kate in North Carolina

Dear Kate,

Thank you for describing so well a common behavior among campers in many activity areas.

Your observation about campers competing for attention is right on target. Children crave the attention of adults and will do whatever seems to work in order to get it. Some children are so desperate for attention that they are willing to do things that result in their getting negative attention—being scolded, getting into trouble, being expelled from an activity, or earning a reputation as a troublemaker.

Whether we are aware of it or not, we adults are always teaching children what to do to gain our attention. All too often these teachings occur unwittingly in a random, knee-jerk fashion, and we end up reinforcing bad habits rather than encouraging more adaptive, productive ones. What helps is when adults are deliberate about teaching children what it is they can do to win our praise and positive attention.

Sit down with your campers before the start of each class and tell them that, from now on, you and the other instructors will not respond to them when they use the phrase, "I can't!" Let them know that you are going to act as if you can't hear them when they say "I can't" or anything that sounds like "I can't" and that, if they want your attention, they will have to be able to use one of the magic phrases.

"What are those magic phrases?" they will want to know. Here's where you will need to be creative. Words like "I'm trying, how's this?" or "Look at me! Watch me do it!" are good choices, because you will notice that they still offer the potential for competing for attention, but in a way that enhances learning.

Once you have had this discussion, be prepared to be tested. You can always count on at least one camper falling back on her bad habit. When this happens, you should prompt the whole group by saying something like, "I can't hear you! What's the magic phrase?" or "You almost forgot! Now, what's the magic phrase?" The more animated and deliberate you are about how you are not listening or responding to the old or unwanted phrase, the more quickly the children will catch on.

Human nature being what it is, I suspect you will see results in a short time if you stick to your plan. Helping a child change her behavior has a lot to do with our thoughtfulness and determination as well as our ability to respond to challenges rather than reacting to the impulsiveness of the average child.

Potpourri of Camp Challenges

1. Children need to be heard.
2. Counselors need to listen for the feeling tone of what campers say, not just content.
3. The "power and control" stage.
4. Using overnight trips for building unity.
5. Group activities build unity.

The busy summer brought fewer letters, but many calls. Here is a sampling from people who were, indeed, in the trenches this summer.

From a day camp in New England comes Skippy. Skippy is a rambunctious, sometimes grumpy seven-year-old who, on his way to swimming one day, sat down and said, "I'm not going!"

The counselor, though perturbed, managed to avoid a tug-of-war. "Are you having a problem with camp, Skippy?"

"I don't think so," he replied. Upon further investigation he revealed, "My parents are going to our summer home and I don't want to go!"

The counselor begins to see Skippy as a selfish kid who just wants his own way and pouts when he doesn't get it.

Unfortunately, children don't often have the words to tell us what is upsetting them. Consequently, they resort to their behavior or refer to some extraneous event to try to convey their grievance. Premature judgment of such behavior can rob us of the chance to help them.

At first glance, Skippy's summer house blues seem not only irrelevant, but irreverent. "Spoiled kids!" thinks the counselor. Yet, what Skippy is giving us is a coded message about how adults don't listen. What Skippy is asking for is to be *heard*. In the rushed world of adults, youngsters often feel passed by and become frustrated when their feelings are not even acknowledged.

The counselor cannot solve the summer home problem, but he or she has an opportunity to give Skippy the gift of listening, from which the fruits of acceptance and validation are born.

To achieve this, have counselors start listening for the *feeling tone* of what campers say, rather than just the content. If Skippy's counselor had done that, here's how the scenario might have proceeded.

1. "Gee, Skippy, you sound angry!" (acknowledging feelings)
2. "No wonder you're upset! It sounds like you're saying that adults don't listen." (labeling feelings)
3. "And no wonder you don't want to go swimming! You probably want someone to start listening to you!" (connecting his behavior empathetically to his feelings)

4. "It must be terrible when adults don't listen." (validating his feelings)
5. "I know how you feel. When people don't listen to me, it makes me hurt and angry too." (sharing one's own experience)
6. "I wonder if your mind isn't getting us mixed up, kind of like your feelings about having to go to your summer home gets mixed up with going swimming." (relating his old experience to his current behavior and distinguishing it from camp)

The boy's response to the last statement is superfluous, because the thrust of this intervention comes from one truth: when children feel heard, they listen.

From the Midwest comes a group of eight twelve-year-old girls participating in a tough experiment in group living. The problem? Constant quarreling, fighting, noncooperation, subgroup competition, and a universal dismissal of the counselor's authority. The girls are stuck in "power and control," a stage of group development all children's groups go through in which the pecking order gets established.

What to do? Talking doesn't help much and moralizing with the girls will only increase their tendency to distance themselves from their counselors. Children tend to solve their problems through activities, and words help only as a way of reinforcing the experience that comes from a team-building activity.

The most effective way to build unity in a group struggling to be together is to take them on an overnight trip. The site need not be far, but it needs to be away from other campers and to include only members of the group. When faced with the task of surviving in the wilderness (regardless of how tame the wilderness might be), petty differences take a low priority.

Make sure you use the nighttime—everyone huddled around a campfire, snug in sleeping bags—to talk. Children are capable of great insight when they are settled down for the evening.

Back at camp, follow up your trip with a cabin party and decorate the cabin together during free periods. There are other group activities that promote unity—camper-counselor water polo (children and adults all float at the same level); friendly competition with another cabin; a special our-cabin-only evening activity, like popping corn over a fire or taking canoes to a nearby island.

Encourage counselors not to give up on the group during this most difficult period. As much as the campers may disparage staff, it is secretly reassuring to them to have counselors who provide activities that help them make the transition from competitive individuals into a more cooperative group.

Being a camp director is a labor of love. These scenes reveal just how difficult it can be to do what is in the best interest of children and camp.

20

Catch Us If You Can

1. Sparring—taking on authority—especially by boys.
2. Boys who spar actually become stronger from imitating, challenging, and testing authority.
3. Young males need sanctioned ways to spar so they don't get into trouble.
4. Some girls like to spar, too.
5. Contact with directors and staff most important to campers.

While visiting a prominent coed camp in the Midwest last summer, I heard about a situation from one of the unit directors that was a classic example of a camper-counselor struggle.

It seems that two young male campers from France, both about fourteen, were getting into a lot of petty mischief. Most of their behavior had a catch-us-if-you-can quality and involved challenging the staff and being provocative with authority. Besides smoking cigarettes and sneaking off from their rooms, the pair routinely evaded their activities and often tried sneaking off campus. "Short of sending them home," asked the unit leader, "is there any other way to work with these two?"

It is important to mention that this unit director had been clear about confronting the boys, had set fair but firm limits, and had spoken to them about sending them home if their behavior did not improve. The boys responded by becoming more clever and devious in their escapades, assuming a "couldn't-care-less" posture with regard to the prospect of being sent home to France. As you might well imagine, most of the counselors and the unit leader were at their wits' ends with the dynamic duo.

What these two boys were doing was what boys everywhere do to some extent. It's called "sparring." Most boys need a way to challenge or take on authority, especially male authority. Through the process of competition and identification, sparring is a way many young males develop a deeper sense of themselves, arrive at a keener sense of fair play (including a clearer sense of right and wrong), and improve their competency and identification. Boys who are naturally drawn to sparring—and not all are—actually become stronger from the imitating, challenging, and testing of authority that this mock fighting provides.

Sparring is a crucial social activity for young males, and, if there are no sanctioned ways for them to have this practice at growing up, they often devise ways of their own that may involve going outside the law. The trick is to provide opportunities for boys to challenge authority without causing them to get into trouble.

This is exactly the position in which the two boys from France found themselves. What they were implicitly doing was looking for a way to challenge and be challenged by the authority at camp. Unfortunately, the only ways they could think of were ways that got them into trouble.

Sparring can take a number of forms and can be as simple as a healthy debate, a keep-away game, water polo, or a chess tournament. The beauty of camp is the wealth and range of activities and opportunities that lend themselves to a healthy form of sparring. For example, we discovered that the two young Frenchmen were good soccer players, so counselors challenged them to recruit a team of campers to take on a counselor team. The dare involved holding practices, scheming about possible plays, and making a lot of noise (posters, pep talks, and verbal challenges, for example) and culminated in a multigame tournament. What it did was siphon the mischievous energy into a healthy, sanctioned public event. And it works!

When you provide an outlet for the natural challenges that campers—and especially adolescents—throw our way, here are some things to keep in mind or to remind your staff about.

1. Don't take the behavior of your campers personally. If their actions get under your skin, you risk losing your perspective and your ability to engage them in constructive activities.
2. Gauge your own moods and feelings. If you are angry, beware of the temptation to get even. Punishment that masquerades as limit setting may only cause resentment and escalate the bad-boy behavior.
3. Choose activities that your campers have some real skill in, thus giving them a sense of having a fighting chance.
4. Many girls like to spar just as boys do. Don't overlook more aggressive or challenging activities for girls who may have needs similar to their male counterparts.
5. Don't be constrained by the limits of your program. By being willing to create something new (like a tournament or special games), you send a powerful message about being flexible and interested in your campers' struggles.
6. Don't purposely lose, but don't drum campers off the field, either. Children, including adolescents, need a chance to get better at beating us. Our job is not necessarily to win or to allow them to win, but to coach them in getting better at taking us on and becoming more skillful in their challenges.
7. Remember, most children are sore winners. So, if they win, they will probably need help in doing so graciously.

One of the most important things to remember is that camp is a contact sport, and the contact that campers crave—of which sparring is only one of many types—is quality time from directors and staff.

Contact with people that is genuine and safe and speaks to the developmental needs of individual campers is the most powerful resource at camp. It is, after all, what your campers all showed up for in the first place, and it is most likely the very force that will bring them back next year.

part two

managing specific behavioral challenges

Homesickness

1. An excursion away from camp helps—campers feel like they are coming home when they come back.
2. Camp sister program—allows older campers to be the experts.
3. Open discussions (as radio show) about homesickness helps.
4. Homesick club.
5. Preparing parents in advance.

Several camp directors have shared their thoughts and ideas with me about campers who miss home that I would now like to share with you.

Pamela Vinicombe, executive director of Murry Grove in Lanoka Harbor, New Jersey, wrote, "I agree with the older brother of a homesick youngster who said, 'Everybody's a *little* homesick!'"

Pamela noted that, in her experience, camper anxiety usually appears the second day of a camp session. Therefore, on the third day of each session, she makes sure an off-campus excursion is planned for at least half a day.

"A hike, a canoe ride, or a town run—anything that separates the campsite from the campers" is what Pamela has in mind. "Thus, when everyone returns, they feel they have 'come home.'"

She added that she arranges for a special drink or snack to be ready for their return as a welcome-back message from the galley. Said Pamela, "Since I have instituted these practices, spirits have been considerably brighter."

Nancy Burns of Waukeela Camp for Girls in Eaton Center, New Hampshire, described what she calls her "Camp Sister" program. (Nancy said she stays away from the words "big" or "little" to avoid any sense of inequality.) Experienced campers are handpicked by Nancy to contact first- or second-year campers.

"They write a letter before camp; some actually meet or have phone conversations. That way, they have a friend at camp before they even get there." Nancy said the program is very popular, and, because she carefully chooses the experienced friends, she's assured of a positive outcome. Contact between camp sisters lasts throughout the summer. Both parties benefit—the newcomers feel more accepted and the old-timers feel useful and gain a true sense of maturity by being experts.

Allowing children to be experts is one of the key strategies we can use that truly makes a difference in working with children, and it is a tremendous aid in working with second-year campers who miss home.

Children are often dismissed by adults as ineffectual or too young to know. When a child is acknowledged by an adult for having experience or know-how that can make a difference, suddenly that child feels important. A child who is busy playing expert has less time to dwell on his or her own homesick feelings.

The use of campers as experts to support newcomers gets an exciting twist at a camp in the Chicago area, where the camp radio station has a daytime show about homesickness. Veteran campers who have been homesick themselves in previous years go on the air to talk about what it was like and how they managed and what they do each summer to get through the first few days of camp.

The greatest gains from this live camper sharing, in addition to helping the veteran who may be missing home, are helping campers realize their feelings are normal and need not be a source of shame and giving permission for everyone at camp to talk openly about feelings. Sharing things that matter not only alleviates sadness, anxiety, and missing home, but also contributes to a sense of community.

Years ago I heard about another way to foster openness at camp. Asher Melzer, a long-time camp professional from New York involved in the Jewish Federation, developed the "homesick club." Asher felt that campers who are homesick have their fears and tears in common and, if helped to share their experiences in a group, might develop rapport and closeness quickly. The homesick club is a positive experience for campers, especially if it involves veteran campers who were homesick as novices.

The beauty of a homesick club is that, by mixing ages and levels of experience (i.e., including first- and second-year homesick campers), not only is the stigma of having homesick feelings reduced, but different members take on different roles in a kind of extended family. For example, a younger first-year camper may support his "brother" in the group, and a girl who misses her sister can adopt another camper to look after or to be with.

The specific problem with second-year homesickness comes from expectations. Everyone seems to think that, by the second year, going away to camp should be easy. Second-year campers may feel that they shouldn't have feelings like this and that, if they admit it, it is admitting a deep and serious flaw.

Kelly Gordon Moxley, program director at Camp Chatuga in South Carolina, sends a letter to parents of returning campers that addresses homesickness. The letter, which is a collection of tips that help a returning camp experience be a great one, mentions possible causes of second-year homesickness—changes at home, upcoming changes at camp, and worries about expectations at camp. The letter even predicts what campers might say in their letters home, such as, "They're making us work!" This helps reduce the possibility of parents being taken by surprise. Having a strong alliance with parents is one of the best defenses against homesickness.

Rob Hammond of Camp Laney for Boys, Mentone, Alabama, plans to send homesick packets to parents of first-year and selected returning campers. "It just makes sense to have parents prepare the boys before they come and for our guidelines to be clear. Besides," said Rob, "parents need reassurance that we are sensitive to their child's needs."

Homesick Veteran Campers

1. Second-year homesickness can be worse than first-year—nobody expects it, so it sneaks up on them.
2. Family situations play a role in homesickness.
3. Exit interviews help set up positive feelings for next year.

Dear Bob,

What can you tell us about homesickness in second-year campers? We feel we do a fair job of preparing for homesickness in first-year campers by working with parents, but are surprised to find the second-year blues to be as much of a problem as they sometimes are.

Surprised in the South

Dear Surprised,

You are one of many camp directors who have identified second-year homesickness as a problem in its own right. Some, like June Gray of Camp Wawenock in Maine, think it is an even more troublesome phenomenon than first-year homesickness because many parents (and counselors) don't expect it, and most children feel they should be over it by their second year at camp. Consequently, children may be harder on themselves and feel more ashamed of their feelings if they are homesick a second year and get less preparation or support from adults who may not expect it.

While it is difficult to answer any question about homesickness in a general way, especially because individual family situations play such an important role in the problem, there are some things you can do. The first is to recognize that most children (and staff) feel ill at ease and somewhat vulnerable *whenever* they make a dramatic change in their environment, even if their feelings are mild and don't last long. As the older brother of a homesick youngster I once saw in my office comforted him, "Most of us miss home at first, Nick—we just don't show it and then we get over it."

The second thing is to keep notes on which campers had difficulty adjusting to camp their first year. This way you can alert parents in the spring to be aware of the phenomenon and even do some preparing of the child before he or she leaves camp for home at the end of his or her first year. I usually do a kind of individualized exit interview with each new camper (or have their counselor do it) to find out what they liked and what they didn't, and then I give them credit for how well they eventually adjusted. This goes a long way in helping a child feel welcome and accepted. It also helps set the stage for you to do what I call "making a prediction." In this case you might mention that you wouldn't be surprised if the child had some minor homesick feelings again next year, because many children do, and that it's a normal part of going away from home and growing up. Also express your confidence in the child's ability to master his or her feelings, just as he or she did this year. Such an approach helps take the stigma off the feelings and makes it easier for a child to accept constructive support. (Remember, children cannot accept help for a problem they feel they shouldn't have in the first place.) You are, in a sense, predicting success rather than setting an expectation for failure.

Going away to camp is a tremendous step for many children, even if it's their third or fourth time doing it, and those of us who have been doing it for a long time can easily underestimate the trepidation a child experiences in the process.

Overcoming Language Barriers among Campers

1. Counselors must be even more involved when some campers are international.
2. Use nonverbal communication.
3. Learn key phrases in language(s) of your campers and have the kids learn words in a game setting.
4. Have American and international campers play together— best for breaking down barriers.
5. Individualized activities in group setting.

Dear Bob,

Over the years we have had an increasing number of foreign campers attend our coed camp in Minnesota. Aside from its being a viable new market, we believe that the presence of foreign campers has made the experience at our camp a richer one for campers and counselors alike.

Occasionally, however, there are problems in cabins where foreign-speaking youngsters sometimes don't mix well with American children. The language barrier seems to keep these cabinmates from developing stronger bonds and closer friendships. Do you have any suggestions about how to help children in this situation get along better?

Diverse in Minnesota

Dear Diverse,

Many camps are enrolling foreign campers in greater numbers with benefits and problems similar to the ones you describe. The most difficult arena does seem to be bunk life, where campers are in close quarters and must work together.

There are several tips to keep in mind when campers from different countries are at camp together. First, the counselor must be prepared to make an even greater effort to be truly present with his or her campers. Cabins that have counselors whose emotional energy and/or physical presence is elsewhere will suffer.

Second, counselors need to use more nonverbal communication, such as a hand on a shoulder, forearm, or upper back (safe touch areas) to get the attention of campers. Staff who primarily use words to get a child's attention need to realize that, in a cabin with campers from a variety of countries, camp is truly a *contact sport*.

Third, counselors who work most closely with mixed groups of campers should learn the phrase, "How do you say...?" in the language of the children in their group. In Spanish, for example, this would be "Como se dice...?" Armed with this simple phrase, a staff member can then ask foreign campers to name key words that he or she can use to make communication more effective. Words such as life jacket, tennis racquet, poison ivy, bumblebee, cleanup, and quiet time can be taught to all of the campers as a sort of game; this will enhance contact between foreign-speaking campers and their English-speaking peers.

Probably the most powerful way to bring campers from different countries together, however, is to have them *play* together. If, as it has been suggested, music is an international language, then play is the universal language of children. When children play together, they laugh; are spontaneous, animated, and resourceful; figure things out together; and discover themes that seem common to all youngsters. The kinds of play I am referring to are simple things, like playing with balloons, playing on swings or playground equipment, digging in the sand, playing with cars, making a dam along a stream, playing in the water, and building something together. Granted, these are not typical camp activities, but they are extremely effective in helping children establish a common ground of understanding and stronger positive feelings for each other.

For a group that is having a particularly difficult time establishing trust, I would suggest doing *individualized* activities in a group setting, such as making something together while listening to music in the background or drawing while listening to music.

Using music to bring children together can be very effective. Children can listen to music together, make a music box (a wooden box onto which several devices that make various percussive noises are attached), learn songs, sing together, or share music from their respective countries. Children who sing together seem to have a harder time hating each other afterwards.

———————

Overheard at camp this summer:

Counselor: "No one told me it was going to be this hard being a counselor! [pause] Well, maybe they did, but I didn't really think I'd be this tired!"

Same counselor (a few days later): "It's really worth it, though, when you see a kid smile and do something they thought they never could do. That's when I feel like I've done something that matters."

Parent of a first-time overnight camper (leaving after visiting day): "It is such a relief to see him with his easy self-confidence, bringing his friends up to introduce us. You realize he really does belong here—he is really thriving! I wish I could bottle this in him and uncork it about halfway through the school year!"

Seasoned camp director: "Why do the children we work with seem to need so much more than they did years ago? Am I just getting older, or is there more to these kids today? I find myself spending a lot of time on marketing and business-related matters. What I *really* want to do is spend more time learning about children. That's why I got into this business in the first place."

32

Bed-Wetting

1. Enuresis
   - diurnal—mostly kids 3–6
   - nocturnal—greatly embarrasses older kids
2. Humiliation—greatest fear.
3. Three categories: a) accidental, b) transitory regression, and c) chronic.
4. No warning from parents. The need for partnering with parents.

I have spoken with and received letters from scores of camp directors regarding bed-wetting.

Bed-wetting, known clinically as enuresis, is a phenomenon that seems highly prevalent at most residential camps. Its daytime version (known as diurnal enuresis) is fairly prominent among younger children (ages three to six) in day camp. Enuresis was voiced as a problem in more than 75 percent of the 200 camps I've visited since 1981. It is not unusual for a child, aged three to five years, to have an accident by not making it to the bathroom on time. Such incidents are part of working with this age group.

At residential camps, however, the situation is different. Children at residential camps are well beyond the daytime accident phase. Older children who wet at night (nocturnal enuresis) are usually more embarrassed by this behavior since they are old enough to recognize that it is not acceptable among their peers. It does not take long for children to become keenly sensitive to anything that might humiliate them. In fact, recent, well-conducted research shows that the single greatest fear children have is of being humiliated. For a youngster, then, bed-wetting can be highly charged and potentially shameful.

Three bed-wetting categories exist.

1. **Accidental.** A one-time occurrence by a child who is tired or overstimulated.
2. **Transitory regression.** A temporary slip backwards, lasting from one to three days, sometimes longer, in a child who has previously mastered bladder control. It is often the result of the excitement or anxiety of leaving home, being in unfamiliar surroundings, or having a new routine.
3. **Chronic.** A child who has never truly mastered nighttime bladder control; can wet from five to seven nights a week, sometimes twice a night.

Given that children feel extremely embarrassed about their problem and are fearful of the ridicule they anticipate if ever found out, counselors need to approach the situation in a sensitive manner. The counselor may approach them by saying, "It must be kind of embarrassing for you. . . ."

In addition, most children will experience relief when counselors put the problem into perspective. In the case of the child who has a one-time accident, this requires an explanation of how such things sometimes happen under unusual conditions and that this is most likely not the beginning of a new, horrific problem. Sharing past experience can help the child know he or she is not the only one to whom this has happened. Making the child responsible for changing his or her own sheets helps keep the situation matter-of-fact and not some crisis that requires special exemptions for the child and extraordinary efforts by the counselor.

At some point, the counselor may need to address the problem of cabinmates. Even if the odor is not apparent, the sheet changing will be noticed and the counselor must be prepared to handle the problem as it arises. Most peers, when given a strong, nonpunitive lead from staff, can be encouraged to refrain from ridiculing a peer.

The matter of the chronic bed wetter is more difficult since the patience of both the counselor and the cabinmates can be severely tried. Many directors instruct staff to regulate the camper's liquid intake after a certain time of day and even advise waking the child throughout the night. I do not recommend this because such maneuvers only cause resentment in both the staff and the child. Furthermore, they are often only intermittently helpful. Most chronic bed wetters are going to stop in their own time. My advice is to live through the problem by "benevolent management." This includes

1. Making sure, in a nonpunitive way, that the child changes his or her own sheets, getting minimal help from staff
2. Making sure campers are well covered on cold nights
3. Not punishing the child for his or her bed-wetting and not forcing him or her to miss out on camp activities or responsibilities

Most directors tell me that many bed wetters arrive at camp without warning from the parents. Parents tell me they withhold such information for several reasons. First, they are afraid that, if a camp knows, it will refuse to accept the child's enrollment. Parents also worry that the information may be shared with some counselors who, in their indiscretion, may humiliate the child. They're also afraid that the child may become furious with them for betraying him or her and revealing this secret. Some parents assume the problem may never surface, so they choose to play it down to allow their child a fresh start.

Camp directors need to reassure parents that the information will be shared only when necessary, and then only with staff who are directly involved. Also, children need to know who knows about their problem, because this makes it easier for them to approach staff.

Some pediatricians have prescribed a trace dose of the drug Tofrinil (imimprimine), for children who bed wet. Tofrinil has an anticholinergic effect in children. This means it makes them less reactive, for example, to bladder pressure, thus allowing their sphincter muscle to maintain bladder control. Clinical studies show it to be 50–65 percent effective in chronic bed wetters. Parents who have a youngster with a bed-wetting problem might wish to consult their family doctor. Tofrinil can often be administered by the nurse as a nasal spray.

Regardless of whether parents choose to use medication or not, the most important goal for directors is creating a safe environment at camp. This includes creating an envelope of emotional safety where feelings are respected and problems are approached in a nonjudgmental fashion. When this environment is created, children and staff alike will flourish.

Scary Stories: Spooking Campers

1. Mental monsters.
2. Mastering fear—practicing in one area (ghost stories) helps master fears in other areas.
3. Know your audience.
4. Moderation is key.

Dear Bob,

We had a camper go home this summer for a reason we've never encountered in our thirty-one years as camp directors. A nine-year-old boy heard a ghost story from one of our counselors. It was so upsetting to him that he developed nightmares that eventually kept him from staying at camp.

His parents were unhappy with us and our counselor, claiming that such a story was inappropriate and likening it to hazing. We think the boy was simply homesick and was using the story as his route home.

Bob, we do not condone hazing or scaring kids and never have. We also recognize that ghost stories are a part of camp tradition. We've never had a problem before, so outlawing them doesn't seem to be the answer. We have our own thoughts about where and how this fits into camp life, but were curious about what ideas you might have.

(Not) Spooked in the Southwest

Dear (Not) Spooked,

Many children beg their counselors to tell them frightening stories or take them on mystery trips. Scary stories offer a chance for children to practice mastering their mental monsters—fears of being away from home, of being alone, of failing and being shamed, and of being overwhelmed by their own impulses. Fun for children is something that strengthens them internally; that is, it's something that adds to their growth and their sense of mastery or of being "big." (Big has a special meaning to a child and, in a psychological sense, means having a greater sense of self.)

Practicing mastery in one area (a scary story) helps children master fears in another. Warding off the monster is an outward manifestation of the inward struggle to master internal monsters.

However, just as children need tasks challenging enough to hold their interest, they also need tasks in small enough doses to lead to success. A story so frightening that it's overwhelming is obviously destructive and has no place in camp.

Camp is a place where a child's growth, sense of well-being, and safety are of primary importance. The essential test of what constitutes mastery versus hazing, therefore, is whether the child has an opportunity for mastery without being overwhelmed.

Some camps have banned ghost stories and mystery rides altogether. Their directors feel there is ample opportunity for mastery, traditions, and camp spirit without having such activities. However, if you feel there is a place for such things at your camp, you need to consider some simple but important factors, beginning with your staff.

Simply giving your counselors guidelines for scary stories is not enough to produce the kind of cooperation you need from them. Two things will get in the way. First, your staff—and this seems especially true of male staff—have their own preconceived notions about what toughens kids up. Second, though most counselors may not admit it, it can be fun to scare campers, even though most counselors don't intend to cause them harm.

My first suggestion is that you encourage your staff to share some of the experiences they've had being scared and doing the scaring. Let the laughter come out. Sharing these real-life experiences will bring your staff closer together and, coincidentally, will provide them with an acceptable outlet—a kind of cathartic release—for whatever unspoken fears or anxieties they may have. In addition, such a discussion will provide you with an opening for educating your staff about fear as mastery and the need for balance and restraint. Once you have done this, provided you have done it without sounding accusatory or judgmental, you can offer your guidelines to a staff that can truly hear what you have to say.

I suggest the following parameters:

1. Know your audience. If there are children in the group who are fearful or overly shy or withdrawn, it would be mean to strain their need for trust. Additionally, younger children have trouble knowing what's real from what isn't, especially at night. Leaving any child confused about what is real is cruel, not funny.
2. Never tell a scary story at the beginning of a session. There isn't enough trust or sense of safety in this new setting to afford the strain of being frightened.
3. Remind your staff that kids may beg for something really scary, but children are often not in a position to choose what is best for them. Moderation is the best policy. The setting of the story should never be at camp or in the town or area in which the camp is situated. Also, the hero or heroine should eventually be victorious. After all, it is mastery that is key here. Why do you think Superman and Batman always win?

Giving youngsters the sense of mastery that they—the smaller, more vulnerable people in the world—crave is what makes camp such a powerful resource for children.

When Campers Tease and Scapegoat

1. Match kids according to maturity level.
2. Reprimanding the group makes it worse for scapegoat.
3. Use bonding activities—keep-away game in water between staff and campers; painting a group mural.
4. All feelings are raw—handling feelings of pride with sensitivity.

Dear Bob,

We often have a problem in some of our camper groups with teasing and ostracism of one child by the others. It seems that this has become almost a perennial problem which some years is quite intense. What can be done to minimize the problem or deal with it more effectively?

Sincere in South Carolina

Dear Sincere,

Scapegoating seems to be a universal phenomenon among children in groups, and, while it probably can never be entirely eliminated, it can be contained with deliberate, but sensitive interventions. Understanding some of the dynamics of the problem may help you to develop a plan for action.

First of all, scapegoating arises out of the specific chemistry of each group, the most common formula being the presence of a child who is clearly more immature than his or her peers (for instance, a clinger or one who cries more easily). One variation of this might be a boy who is either more aggressive in an immature way (hits or bites, for example) or more constricted in regard to aggressive impulses (e.g., afraid to take normal risks; overly shy or fearful) than his peers. The first defense against scapegoating, then, is more careful matching with respect to maturity levels.

When scapegoating does arise, however, it is a tough problem with no easy answers. I have found that, even though the scapegoated child may elicit our sympathies, it is a mistake simply to reprimand the children who are the aggressors. Such a course of action only heightens the resentment of the group toward the scapegoat, who will pay dearly for it once the adults are off the scene.

One of the subtle but crucial dynamics to understand about scapegoating is the use by the victimized child of his or her helplessness to gain special favor from the staff. In fact, the hidden drama occurring between the scapegoat and the popular leader of the group is their covert struggle to be special, vying for the secret affections of counselors

38

(or other adult authorities). This is why the problem gets worse when there is a vacuum created by the absence of staff.

The best antidote for scapegoating is the active, creative involvement of counselors with the group in activities that force the members of the group to unite. One good example is a keep-away game in the water between counselors who supervise the group and all the kids. Playing in the water is especially effective because children float at the same level as adults, meaning that instantly everyone is on a par with everyone else, both symbolically and in some real physical way.

However, you may need to help your staff be aware of two important dangers—one is that the group will attempt to reject the scapegoat by trying to put him or her on the side with the counselors. Warn your staff not to go along with such a maneuver since it only perpetuates their rejection of the child and, ironically, serves to increase their resentment of the child. The other danger is that your staff may misinterpret their job as one of beating the kids or letting the kids win. Neither is true. Their job is to make the kids *work* at winning, keeping the game within reach, but always coaching the kids about ways they can improve their chances (like developing better teamwork).

Other activities that bring a group closer together include painting a group mural, taking the counselors on in building a sand castle or other competitive construction project, or anything that requires the group to pull together as a team (not necessarily a sports activity). Avoid such things as water-balloon or squirt-gun fights, however, since they are too stimulating at this stage and may provoke a fight or injury.

On a separate track, when a scapegoating problem exists, it is important to remember that, no matter how disguised, everyone's feelings are raw. Children, like adults, need to save face. Indicting them does not teach acceptance or empathy. Talk with the group in a general, nonjudgmental way about the importance of each individual's pride and the need to find ways for each member to shine and make a contribution to the group.

At times it is effective to say to a boy who is being victimized, with his attackers present, "You know why these guys are teasing you. They're trying to 'toughen' you up! They'd like to see you be able to be tougher and more grown up!" Reframing the group's abusive behavior in the best possible light (which has a truth to it previously unseen by the children themselves) opens the way for a leader to invite the group to think of less punitive ways for them to help the kid grow up.

As soon as the group knows that they are not going to be treated punitively—even though certain of their behaviors will not be condoned—they can join in a more tolerant, cooperative spirit. However, staff members need to continue to offer fun, challenging activities, with their involvement as a channel for their campers' aggressive feelings and a forum for mastery, success, team spirit, and positive contact with adults.

Opportunities for Success

1. Bullies have low self-worth and self-confidence.
2. Brainstorm with staff about what they've noticed about bullies.
3. Bullies pick on younger, smaller kids and can dish it out but can't take it.
4. Help bullies experience success—encourage, support, coach, and praise them.
5. Channel bullies into confidence-building activities.

Dear Bob,

Last summer, we had some trouble with a couple of boys who taunted, teased, and generally picked on some of the other campers. We set clear limits with both boys, but we were not always able to catch them in the act of bullying. What suggestions do you have for working with such youngsters?

New York State of Mind

Dear New York,

Most bullies suffer from a low sense of self-worth and a lack of deep-down self-confidence. While I think it is important to set limits on such behavior, policing such youngsters does not address the condition that causes bullying. There are some practical, simple things we can do at camp to help bolster the self-esteem of children who feel the need to tease others.

Since counselors are faced with working with these youngsters on a daily basis, my first suggestion is to enlighten and empower the staff to do the intervening work. Start by brainstorming with your counselors about what they have noticed about children who bully other children. I suspect the list you generate will include the following:

1. They can dish it out, but they can't take it.
2. They usually pick on younger, smaller, or more vulnerable kids.
3. They don't have much self-confidence, a fact they hide by taking aim at the weaknesses or mistakes of other children.

Brainstorming gets your staff focused, helps them be more reflective, and gives you an opportunity to engage them as problem solvers in a positive way. Developing this position with the staff helps them to be less *reactive* to difficult children and encourages them to be more *responsive*. Given that bullies and other challenging youngsters have a way of getting under our skin, it is important to help staff avoid the potential to be punitive or impulsive.

unit one
camper behavior

Once you have enlisted the staff, the next step is to find out what the child likes to do or wants to do at camp. Since most children want to have fun and experience success, this won't take much effort. Focus on one or two activities and speak with the counselors that teach or supervise those activities. Have them welcome the youngster; encourage, support, and coach him; and report back verbally to the child's cabin counselor. Cabin counselors can then reinforce the success of the child and provide additional praise, encouragement, and other positive attention. This team approach can work wonders in just a few days.

Remember that bullies are children who do not have much "money" in their personal "banks," so they go about making "deposits" in counterfeit ways by preying on other kids in a vain attempt to bolster their own "accounts" or status. If we can give them bona fide ways to feel good about themselves—to make deposits in the bank of self-esteem— we lessen their need for acting out.

41

Enforcing Appropriate Behavior

> When a camper overreacts to teasing and threatens another:
> 1. The child must acknowledge breaking a camp rule.
> 2. The child must see that there are other ways to respond to teasing.
> 3. Use contracting.
> 4. Use of violence not acceptable at camp.

Dear Bob,

We had an episode at camp last summer that caused quite a stir. An eleven-year-old boy (whom I'll call Tom) had been teased by another boy (whom I'll call Roy). Tom left Roy's cabin, went to his own, and got a knife that he had brought to camp without anyone's knowledge. Possessing a knife in camp is against our rules.

Luckily, on the way back to Roy's cabin, Tom was intercepted by a counselor. My question is, does Tom go home or does that preclude us from being able to help a youngster who may truly need it? Our staff was quite divided on this issue.

Troubled

Dear Troubled,

The ideal response to your camper Tom would be to keep him at camp and send his knife home. However, you must determine whether or not you can help this boy before considering if he should stay.

Here are some key factors you must consider. If, after you have confiscated the knife and Tom has had a chance to cool off, he can recognize that he has broken a camp rule by having a knife at camp and that he was acting in an unacceptable way by getting the knife instead of getting some help, then you have something to work with. If the boy cannot see that he acted inappropriately by bringing a knife into camp and attempting to use it to settle a score (even if he meant only to threaten someone with it), then you have nothing else to do but call the parents and relate the incident to them. At this point I would also make a strong recommendation to the parents that they get the boy some help, because this kind of behavior is a clear cry for intervention.

So step one is to have the boy acknowledge that he broke a camp rule. Step two is to have the boy acknowledge that there are other ways that he could have responded to the teasing and to have him identify a counselor with whom he has some kind of positive relationship to whom he can go when needed.

The third step is what is known as "contracting." Contracting is simply making an agreement with a camper and formalizing it by writing it down on paper. It should be signed by the camper, the director, and a counselor trusted by the camper. The contract should state that the camper agrees to talk to someone when he has been hurt or teased or otherwise feels angry about something someone has done to him. The contract should specify a particular counselor for the boy to seek out when he needs to talk. Allow the boy to contribute to the contract by designating a counselor of his choice.

The other provision of the contract is a promise by the camper not to resort to any kind of threat or violence in the future at camp. The idea, of course, is to reinforce the notion that using a stick, stone, or weapon to settle a grudge is simply not acceptable at camp. To help accomplish that goal, other outlets or means of expressing feelings and resolving conflicts such as time-outs must be provided.

If the youngster can agree to the steps I have outlined, you have the makings of an important lesson for a young man who needs it. Remember that children are not born civilized—we must guide them to make them that way.

Contracting with Campers

1. Contracting with campers is an effective, practical tool for achieving success with challenging camper behavior.
2. Some contracts with returning campers can be drawn up before campers arrive at camp.
3. Successful "camper agreements" incorporate these features:
   - enlists parental support and approval
   - confirms that the child does, indeed, want to be at camp
   - targets specific behaviors
   - establishes positive and negative consequences
   - has camper sign agreement
4. Good agreements require follow-up and adjustments.

Dear Bob,

Last summer we had a camper returning for her third year whose reputation for being disruptive and challenging seemed to get to camp before she did. The counselors who discovered that this girl was going to be in their group were upset and visibly concerned about their ability to work with her in a productive way even before she arrived.

Just as we expected, this young lady created havoc in her bunk. She started rumors about other girls in her unit, played one girl against another, made derogatory comments about counselors and campers, and was often accused of taking things from others without asking. We tried lots of different approaches, including talking with her, having long bunk discussions, and bringing other girls together to confront her, but nothing really seemed to work. It was also very difficult at times to prove whether she had, indeed, taken something or not, as accused by the other girls.

Do you have any ideas about how to handle such children, who seem to take an inordinate amount of time from the other campers and who seem to be so upsetting and challenging to counselors?

Nervous in New York

Dear Nervous,

The situation you describe is all too common at many camps. From the sound of it, the young lady you describe is either a preadolescent or early adolescent teen. Teens can be especially challenging to work with because of their tendency to be, at times, rebellious, stridently independent, or aloof.

It sounds to me as if this young lady is already on what I call the "third page," or the third level of intervention. Appealing to her sense of justice or community and having talks with her and the other girls probably is not enough medicine to treat her particular problems. This is a young lady who needs to be involved in some kind of agreement or contract before she sets foot in camp. A lot of people use contracting with campers, but I want to walk through the steps that I think make contracting especially powerful.

Step 1. Work with the parents: First, discuss the agreement with the camper's parents. If the presentation is made in a sensitive way and framed in terms of "helping your daughter have the most success she can at camp," most parents are not only cooperative, but grateful that someone is willing to work on a deeper level with their child. Assure the parents that the contract will be kept as confidential as possible, with only the child, her bunk counselor, the unit director, and the camp director being involved. Explain that the child will be actively involved in drawing up the agreement and that there will be positive consequences for successful behavior, as well as very clear negative consequences for undesired behavior.

Once you have involved the parents, you are ready to proceed to the second step in the contracting process.

Step 2. Include the camper: Some children balk at the word "contract," so you must determine whether you are going to call the agreement a contract or an agreement. Start the process by talking directly with the girl. If you can do this in person, it will be more effective, although you can negotiate the arrangement easily over the phone.

- Begin by explaining to the camper that you want her to be as successful at camp as she can be. Do not be shy about pointing out that you know that she has had some difficulties in the past, but that you expect she has done a year of growing. Tell her that you want to believe in her and have her succeed and have fun at camp.
- Then introduce the idea of having an agreement in place before she comes to camp. Tell her that this will ensure the best time possible at camp. Explain that you have spoken to her parents and that they are in full agreement with this process and arrangement.

The actual substance of the contract should be very simple. You should identify between one and three things that you want this girl to be able to do while she is at camp. These behaviors should be very specific, since generalities lead to confusion, misunderstandings, and failure. The specific target behaviors should be stated in the agreement in positive terms. For instance, in the case of the girl you described, I would target three items or behaviors for compliance and state them as follows:

1. The girl should say only nice things about fellow campers.
2. She should first ask permission before taking or borrowing something from another camper.
3. She should talk with her counselor if she is upset or has any difficulties with other campers in her bunk.

Stating things this way avoids any arguments about spreading rumors, stealing, or being mean to campers. Stating the terms positively helps you stay on the path to success while keeping the process from being controversial, argumentative, or adversarial. Remember, you are trying to create an alliance with a girl who does not enter such alliances easily or with much trust.

During the process of working out the specific target behaviors, ask the girl frequently if she clearly understands what these behaviors are. Does she understand what is being asked of her and what she has to do to comply?

Step 3. Establish consequences: This step establishes the positive and negative consequences that accompany the arrangement.

- *Positive consequences* should be worked out in partnership with the camper. For example, she might suggest two or three different things that she would like to earn or be able to do as a result of complying with the terms or her agreement. Some possible rewards: getting extra tickets or credits for the canteen, being able to go water skiing an extra time, or earning a special treat or activity for her group. Insert different positive consequences for different time frames. For example, the camper might be able to participate in a special activity if she is successful for the first half day.
- You need to have regular check-ins at specified time intervals. Note in the agreement that the time periods are flexible. Some children have more immediate success and others need more prompting or shorter trial periods. Feasible positive consequences require creativity, imagination, and the ability to include the camper in the process.
- *Negative consequences* should be established for noncompliance. For example, if after the first half day the camper has been making rude comments or is being mean to campers, as reported by her counselors, she might be put on probation. Probation would be a first warning step. If the behavior persisted, she might have to sleep in the health center (of course, whatever is done must be safe and supervision must be guaranteed), she might lose certain privileges, or she might have to call home to tell her parents what she has done. A third level of negative consequences would exist if the girl persisted in misbehaving even after being placed on probation and losing additional privileges.

I believe that, if children cannot comply with these arrangements, they are telling us they are not able to be present at camp. The child must know that she can stay at camp only if she is really willing to work toward success. The parents must also know of this condition from the beginning of the process. If the child's behavior tells you she does not want to be at camp, you will be able to follow through on sending her home.

Step 4. Sign the agreement: The final step in the process is having everyone, including the camper, sign the contract or agreement in the presence of the camper's counselor, unit director, and (if necessary) the camp director. This must be done as soon as possible after she arrives at camp. Reiterate that everyone expects and hopes that the camper will be successful and that everyone will work with her to try to guarantee her success. However, you must also make it very clear that the final outcome, in terms of her success, really depends on her efforts.

Usually, when counselors know that a child is already part of an agreement that has been negotiated with the parents and the camper, they relax because they feel they have some recourse to challenge negative behavior.

Contracting is a very strong form of intervention and should be used only when other attempts at managing behavior have failed. Many camps have very clearly and carefully taken this step-by-step process and have been successful. I have found that parents are often grateful for the camp professionals' willingness to take these extra and very professional steps toward helping their child. Very often, if the camper does have success, it will influence other areas of her life.

47

Time Out for Time-Outs

1. Warning of a time-out may be all that is necessary.
2. Specify the unwanted behavior and ask if child wants a time-out.
3. If child acknowledges the misbehavior, give praise.
4. A way of teaching consequences, which is first step in development of a moral code.

Dear Bob,

In a session I attended at the 1990 ACA National Conference, you and Dr. Nancy Cotton made a strong case for using time-outs as a disciplinary measure with younger children. I often find that children simply need an activity other than the one they're involved in to settle down.

Since parents pay good money to send children to camp, it doesn't make sense to have them spending valuable time sitting on the sidelines. I feel that camp is too important for children to miss. Could you comment on this?

Linda Shapiro
Ivy League Day Camp
Smithtown, New York

Dear Linda,

Distracting children by offering other activities that better catch their imagination is a way of intervening with difficult children that is certainly appropriate. Many children display overly aggressive or selfish behavior—not sharing, taking things from other children, being impatient and demanding, and so on—especially at the beginning of camp, as a way of expressing their insecurity or anxiety. Offering alternative activities can help appease or reassure children and make them feel more comfortable in their new environment.

I see time-outs, however, as an important way of giving children the beginnings of moral reasoning by letting them know in a clear, yet benevolent, way that certain behaviors are unacceptable.

The presence of a friendly, helpful, reassuring staff member who is clear about unwanted behavior from the start of camp goes a long way toward minimizing such behavior. If a staff person can enter the child's world and be clear about what is expected, time-outs will be used sparingly. If children are spending too much valuable time sitting on the sidelines, as you put it, something is wrong with the staff or you have an unusually difficult group of children. (In the case of the latter, time-outs can be extremely effective, especially if combined with careful programming and parental involvement.)

I find that a time-out is often unnecessary if a warning is issued first. For this to be effective, the staff member must address the child by his or her first name, then state the unwanted behavior clearly, and then state the warning about a time-out. You might say, "Tommy, if you keep taking clay from others without asking, you might have to take a time-out."

I also find that asking the child if he or she is *asking* for a time-out can help the child bring his or her behavior under control. I might say, "Tommy, are you asking me for a time-out? By taking clay from other children when you know you're not supposed to, it makes me think you're asking for a time-out. Is that right?" If the child says "no," ask what he or she must do to avoid the time-out. Praise the child when he or she gets it right. If a child complies after the warning, praise should also be given.

So far, we have specified the unwanted behavior, and we have asked the child to acknowledge it. We use praise when we get the right response.

Only after all these moves have failed should a time-out be used. At this point, the time-out should be announced by using the child's first name, repeating the unwanted behavior, stating what the desired behavior is, and then assigning the time-out. (Some people prefer to tell a child they can return whenever they can display the desired behavior, but I think the child has already shown an unwillingness to display the appropriate behavior.)

Time-outs are a way of teaching consequences, which is the first step in the development of a moral code.

The length of the time-out will not mean much to the child. What is important is that the time-out takes place. In this way, you can minimize the actual number of minutes any child spends on the sidelines.

Parents *do* want their children to be as fully engaged at camp as possible. It may take special work with parents for them to know that time-outs are an important way of teaching children and that they can be used sparingly, with minimal interruption in their child's day.

49

Telling Tales

1. Children tattle to solidify their position with the staff.
2. Children need reassurance that they do belong—devise a special job for them to help you rather than tattling.
3. Children often practice their newly gained sense of morality by identifying other culprits (righteous indignation).

Dear Bob,

I'm wondering why it is that children like to tell tales. How should we respond when they do? If a camper runs and tells a counselor that Johnny is climbing a tree he shouldn't be climbing, how should the counselor react? Thanking the camper for his concern about Johnny may reinforce snitching behavior which isn't always a good thing (although, in principle, such concern is good). On a practical level, it is hard for the counselor to ignore Johnny's misbehavior once it has been brought to his attention.

Scott Compton
Douglas Ranch Camps

Dear Scott,

I take it that what you mean by "telling tales" is, in Americanese, tattling or being a tattletale. There are two different reasons for this behavior. It would be wise to determine which reason is activating the behavior as this will determine your strategy for responding.

The most common motive for tattling is to gain favor with and approval from adult authority. Younger, less mature, or more insecure children will often tattle to solidify their position with a counselor in a kind of sibling rivalry with other campers.

The task is to reassure these children that they do indeed belong. You can perhaps devise a special way for them to help you out other than tattling. Once you have come up with this special job, you can have a gentle, but clear, private talk where you say three things.

1. You understand they are trying to help out by telling on the other children, but
2. looking after campers is *your* job, and
3. you want them not to tell on other children, but to help you by doing their special job with you.

When tattlers goof, as they inevitably will, and tell on someone again, invoke the memory of this conversation by saying something like, "Oh, you almost forgot! Remember our special agreement—what we said about telling?" Then repeat the three points you told them earlier.

unit one
camper behavior

The second reason a child tells tales has to do with his or her own shaky or newly attained impulse control. A child previously tempted to misbehave practices his or her new morality by identifying other culprits. It is as if the child is saying, "See, I'm not like that—I'm good!" This moral outrage at others' misbehavior tends to be exercised more by boys, whose aggressive physical behavior has historically gotten them into trouble.

These children need reassurance about their own capacity to be good. I sometimes respond, "Thank you, Jimmy, for telling me. You and I know that you would never do something like that. Perhaps Tommy needs my help to figure out how he can be good because he's still learning how." The moral outrage stage is a passing one that can be made shorter by allowing the child success not only in helping out, but also in being socially successful with other campers.

In each case I make it clear to the child that I or another counselor will take care of the youngster who is being told on. When making an intervention, I make sure the tattler is not in tow.

Camper Carvings—Saying Goodbye

1. Kids want to have a record of their presence
   - will I be missed/remembered?
   - will I hold on to my memories?
2. The more insecure children are, the more they want to leave a mark.
3. Teach campers how to say goodbye.
4. Provide sanctioned alternatives: totem pole, plaque, mural; give them things they can take with them or leave behind.

Dear Bob,

We've had a problem with campers cutting their initials into bunks or using markers to inscribe their names. We've spoken to counselors and campers alike, but with varying degrees of success. There seem to be some campers who manage to get their initials or names into their bunks before they leave no matter what we do. After many years this can be quite a problem. We're interested in your thoughts.

Partners in Crime Prevention

Dear Partners,

Children often seek concrete ways of establishing a record of their experience or presence at camp.

When children experience a significant event in their lives such as they do at camp, there are several pressing issues that surface as that experience comes to a close. The major themes for children can be reduced to two essential issues: Will I be missed/remembered? Will this experience remain with me?

For most children at camp these urgent questions remain unarticulated and, therefore, often unanswered. The area most directors need to develop more fully is the process of preparing campers and counselors to say "goodbye." Since children don't always have words for such profound matters, they need help.

Children who are not helped to express their concerns or wishes appropriately will devise their own methods. Campers want to know they will be remembered, that they make a difference, that their time at camp was special. Some campers may feel that putting their initials on the bunk is a way of marking their presence and proclaiming their spot to successive generations.

The more uncertain children are about their value or identity, the more they are prone to resort to more concrete ways of leaving their mark. Adolescents, who often feel under siege and experience a tremendous upheaval with regard to their identity, write their names on just about anything they can find (notebooks, sneakers, each other, and so on). By putting their mark everywhere, they can counteract their fear of fading away or being lost to history. Boys at camp, especially adolescents, tend to be more enchanted than their female counterparts with carving their initials into things. Females in our culture are more adept and supported in their efforts at acknowledging the importance of relationships in their lives. Thus, when camp comes to a close, females tend to be more open and direct about the importance of their bonds and have therefore developed a richer set of rituals with which to express concerns and feelings about endings. One could say that, where girls sometimes share by crying, singing, and talking, boys share by building and carving.

So what can you do? First of all, harness the natural tendencies children have to make tangible artifacts of their experience by providing them with sanctioned opportunities—like a totem pole for carving their names and initials or plaques to be hung in a special place (some kids prefer to leave a painted hand print or do a mural). Other concrete symbols of the impact of camp include pictures and awards, armbands, special bandanas, hats, flags, shirts (one for each bunk with the counselors, kids, and year), or just about anything that kids can take with them or leave behind. One group of campers I worked with from a day camp for emotionally disturbed children decided to dig up a sapling in the woods and plant it, with a plaque they made, on the camp's grounds in memory of their time there.

You can also hold ceremonies that address the value of each child's presence and the value of the community each child helped create. In this setting, group sharing about what was fun, what was new, and what was growth can have tremendous impact on a child's memory of camp. Children need help with the words, and vespers and campfires are places of passing on such culture.

Third, but most important, are the talks counselors have with campers, preferably in their bunks (or, at day camp, in their cubbies). This is the arena for sharing memories and talking about what was good and not so good, what never happened or was not finished, and what will be missed as well as what will be taken along (e.g., memories, friendships, skills, abilities, new ways of coping). Children need both the words—the opportunity to share their thoughts and feelings—as well as the objects and activities (like a celebration) that mark their time at camp.

The more children are left with their feelings unexpressed, the stronger will be their need to resort to their own devices. Camp is a highly charged, intense slice of life for most children. Human beings are symbolic animals who need to mark our experiences in some lasting way. Camps need to provide children and staff with ample opportunities to remember all that camp has been. Having this means of expression, your campers will be less likely to forget you.

53

part three
syndromes and discrete disorders

Aliens in Alabama

> 1. ADD kids are not psychotic, lazy, willfully destructive, or looking for attention; they can't control their ADD.
> 2. Kids can only use the words they know to describe what's happening to them.
> 3. Ritalin isn't a tranquilizer or sedative; it is water soluble, quickly metabolized, and in summer—when kids are more active and it's hotter—dosage may need to be increased.
> 4. It is not better to tire out an ADD kid than give a drug.
> 5. Getting information from parents, doctors, and camp doctors is key.

Dear Bob,

This summer we had an eleven-year-old boy at camp whose behavior required us to send him home early—something we rarely have to do. This young fellow had a very difficult time settling down, especially at meals, during rest hour, and in the evening. During meals he would throw things, constantly be out of his seat, have trouble keeping his hands to himself, and so on. By the end of the meal, he would have the negative attention of his entire group.

Whenever confronted, the boy was genuinely contrite and sincere in his desire to improve. It seemed to us that his impulses just got the best of him. By the end of ten days the boy, who by this time had made most of his peers uneasy, began talking about a "demon possession," saying that "aliens from outer space" were invading his body and making him do bad things.

We prefer enabling our campers to adjust and stay at camp, but "aliens from space" are out of our league, Bob. Any thought you can share would be appreciated.

By the way, the boy's parents told us that he had something called "attention deficit disorder," which affects his ability to concentrate in school, and he takes Ritalin for it during the school year.

Alarmed by Aliens in Alabama

Author's note: There has been a lot of confusion over the labeling of behavior known today as "attention deficit hyperactive disorder" (ADHD). The confusion is the result of ever-emerging new data and understanding of the syndrome. In the early 1970s the series of behaviors we call ADHD today was known as "minimal brain dysfunction" (MBD). Then it became known simply as "hyperkinesis" or hyperactivity. Eventually, this evolved into "attention deficit disorder" (ADD). Today, experts see various forms of ADD—some with and some without hyperactive behavior. In other words, one can be inattentive and calm or inattentive and hyperactive. Attention deficit hyperactive disorder (ADHD) refers to the syndrome that includes hyperactivity. Attention deficit disorder (ADD) may either be someone using an outmoded label, or it may refer to the syndrome without hyperactivity. (In other words, many mental health professionals are confused, too.) Furthermore, there can be subtypes (such as distractable type and residual) with hyperactivity.

Dear Alarmed,

The key to this boy's problems are in your last paragraph concerning the attention deficit disorder and Ritalin.

While there has been much new clinical and empirical research on ADD, most parents and professionals are not knowledgeable about the subject and still tend to operate under several misconceptions.

Your letter is timely because more and more children are going to camp either on Ritalin or with a history of taking it during the school year. Without going into an exhaustive explanation, let's look at some key points.

Misconception #1: Children with ADD are lazy, psychotic, willfully destructive, or looking for attention.

While your camper's demon possession may have seemed quite bizarre to his peers and your staff, this boy is not crazy—he's merely describing what life, in fact, is like for him. Remember that children often lack words to describe their experience in a precise way, so they do it the only way they know how.

For a child who feels in control one moment, only to be overwhelmed by sensory input the next, his saying that he is being "invaded by aliens" is a kind of code that represents his experience of being like two different people, one of which is alien to him.

Misconception #2: Children with ADD could, if they really tried, control it.

To understand the fallacy of this belief, you need a crash course in what is believed to be at the core of ADD and its more severe cousin, hyperactivity (hyperkinesis).

All of us have a kind of mental switchboard that controls sensory input—the sights, sounds, smells, associations, and memories that all compete for our attention. Certain hormones in the brain help select out, or attend to, more important thoughts, feelings, and sensations while disregarding the rest. This is what enables us to track ideas, follow things to their logical conclusions, be organized, not be distracted, and even finish a sentence.

Youngsters with ADD evidently produce less of these naturally occurring hormones, or inhibitors, resulting in disorganization, an inability to follow through on good intentions, and a variety of other disruptions of attention that vary in intensity, depending on how serious the case is. They may look like bad kids, but they usually can't help what they do.

Try as they might, children cannot be willful about how much of a particular hormone their brains produce. ADD is not simply a glorified attention-getting disorder.

Misconception #3: Ritalin is a tranquilizer or sedative; Ritalin is addictive.

Although it would be logical to assume that a child who has difficulty settling down might benefit from a tranquilizer, that is not what Ritalin is. It is thought that Ritalin speeds up the production of the inhibiting hormones mentioned earlier that most people produce naturally. Without the benefit of these hormones, a child is bombarded with more information than he can handle, resulting in severe distractibility, disorganization, impulsivity, and overstimulation. It is this overstimulation that makes a youngster look like he or she might need a tranquilizer or downer.

Ritalin is a water-soluble, highly metabolized drug with few side effects (some children, however, report changes in appetite, stomach upset, and fatigue). What this means is that a standard dosage (from 5 milligrams [mg] to 25 mg at a time) doesn't last very long in the summer, when children are more active and the weather is warmer. Increased perspiration may mean a child is sweating the drug out of his or her system more quickly, requiring an adjustment in the dosage. (Obviously, a physician should be consulted on this.) Ritalin is not habit-forming or addictive.

Misconception #4: ADD mostly affects a child's performance in school.

The youngster you describe would probably have benefited tremendously at camp from the help that Ritalin can offer. (Of course, the drug must be prescribed by a physician.) Making friends, being mindful of the needs of others, being able to wait, and especially being aware of the consequences of actions are subject to attention, organization, and sorting-out stimuli just as much as are learning to add a column of numbers or holding onto a thought while finishing a paragraph. Not being able to attend to stimuli in a manageable way puts your camper at a terrible disadvantage.

Misconception #5: Tiring out a hyperactive child or one with ADD is better than giving him or her a drug.

The truth is, running down a hyperactive kid or one with ADD makes for a tired child who can't sit still or pay attention. Remember, when used effectively, Ritalin is not like drugging a child; it is merely giving them the same advantage of increased power of attention that the rest of us enjoy. Whether any particular child with ADD or hyperactivity can effectively function at camp without Ritalin should be discussed with a pediatrician or child specialist.

The following are some practical tips to employ when you discover you have a child with ADD or hyperkinesis who is on Ritalin.

1. Get a history of the child's behavior on and off the drug, in person or over the phone, from the parents.
2. If the child is on Ritalin during the school year but will not be taking it at camp, find out whose decision that is—the parents' or the prescribing physician's. Some doctors allow parents to elect drug "holidays" for their kids. Some children can handle this, while for others Ritalin is not an elective aid.
3. Get permission to speak to the prescribing doctor about the child and about whether Ritalin would be helpful to the child in adjusting to camp life. Such permission should be a routine condition of accepting a child at camp who is on Ritalin.
4. Talk with your own camp physician or child psychiatrist to get more information about ADD, hyperactivity, and Ritalin.
5. For further information on ADD, write to

> National Attention Deficit Disorder Association
> PO Box 972
> Mentor, OH 44061
> 800/487-2282

Getting more information on topics like ADD and Ritalin is part of the ongoing education of a responsible camp director in a complex and modern world. If you are not using such knowledge now, you will be soon.

58

Working with Highly Active Campers

1. Three to five percent of American school children have ADD/ADHD or are on Ritalin.
2. Hyperactivity can be nonclinical—just from excitement or anxiety—or clinical—from ADD or trauma, or by being overstimulated.
3. Need more frequent and immediate feedback—positive preferred.
4. Be firm and clear, not mean. Prompt and reward.
5. Cooling-off time after activities.

Dear Bob,

Every summer we have a number of campers who have an extraordinary level of energy. Some people call these children hyperactive; others just say they are overenthusiastic.

My question concerns my staff, who, after all, are the ones who work with these campers every day. What advice can you give us about working with these children?

Practical Camp Director

Dear Practical,

You are not alone in your concern about highly active campers. In addition to generally enthusiastic youngsters, camps across the country reported an increase in the number of children enrolled last summer either with the diagnosis of ADD/ADHD or on Ritalin (or some similar medication). Indeed, about 3 to 5 percent of American school children have an attention deficit disorder of some type, and more and more of them are coming to camp.

Many children can, from time to time, act hyperactive. Hyperactivity can be caused by many nonclinical factors—excitement about being at camp or at a favorite camp activity; anxiety about being away from home or in the company of people who are not yet quite friends; nervousness about performing in a new activity.

There are also clinical reasons for a child's overactive behavior. These include

1. Having an attention deficit disorder that is organic (based in the brain)
2. Having had a trauma (death of a parent or divorce, for example), from which a child has not yet recovered

3. Being overstimulated by highly charged material or information (which may or may not be sexual in nature—like having seen an X-rated video)

It is important for counselors to know whether a camper has a true attention deficit disorder, since children with ADD/ADHD often exhibit behavior that is *not* willful, such as not listening, messing up on rules that were just talked about, or going ahead without permission of the staff. In other words, campers with ADD/ADHD are not simply being defiant or consciously misbehaving; they are showing the effects of their disorder. These campers need a different kind of *partnership* with a counselor, since they often have trouble paying attention, keeping track of the rules, knowing what is expected of them, and so on.

Another reason to know who does and who does not have an organically based hyperactivity problem is that some children who look hyper may be sending us a coded message that is actually a cry for help. In some cases the help is for better self-control, while in other cases it may be a sign that a child is struggling with an emotional injury with which he or she cannot cope on his or her own.

The good news is that, at camp, most of the same approaches and strategies that work with campers who have ADD/ADHD can be used successfully with all campers who are highly active. For example, most youngsters with ADD/ADHD need more frequent and more immediate feedback from counselors than other children. They need to know when they are doing well and when they are about to go astray or do something not so well. On the other hand, *all* campers can benefit from that kind of feedback.

Children with ADD/ADHD also respond better when the feedback is positive; when the instructions are simplified; when commands and rules are stated positively (when they are told *what* to do as opposed to what *not* to do); and when the counselor makes better eye contact with them or uses light, appropriate, *reassuring* touch, like a hand on the shoulder. All of these tactics would work just as well with children who are highly active—or with most campers in general.

The single greatest difference between campers who have ADD and those who do not is that children who *can* control their behavior if they try need to get help being accountable for their actions. In other words, the counselor must begin to focus on helping a child take control of him- or herself. One of the ways to do this is to stress clearly and simply what your expectations as a counselor are and then to be equally clear about consequences. For children who do not have an organically based problem, and even for children who can gain *better* control with some effort on their part, such things as earning privileges, losing a privilege, or taking a time-out are effective strategies. Remember that your goal as a counselor is to help children master new behavior. If this means being firm—and you can be firm without humiliating a child—

then, even if they are angry with you, you can help them do some good growing up.

Once you are clear that being *firm* is not being *mean*, you can take a look at some other strategies that help with children who are highly active. For example, in the bunk or with the group, have the rules stated clearly and post them so campers can see them. Keep the rules simple. Have campers repeat them back to you so you can confirm that they understand what is expected. Put your commands and rules in positive terms. Break tasks down into smaller steps so they are easier to follow.

Prompt campers with what you want from them. That means giving them a hint or suggestion *before* they do something. With very active campers, using rewards works, but you will find that you will have to change the reward frequently, since highly active children get bored quickly with whatever you use as the prize. Try rewards like a special time with you, special time doing a favorite activity, or the opportunity to help out with something fun—like helping to light the campfire that night or blowing the whistle at a game. Good supervision in anything you do with an active child is essential.

Many highly active children need a cooling-off time after a strenuous activity. If they don't get such a moment, they can become irritable and end up in a fight. When coming to the end of an activity period, give the group a several-minute warning that the activity is about to come to a close. This helps everyone get used to the idea that they will have to stop and put things away. Keep highly active children nearer to you—the closer they are, the easier you can see when they are about to "go off" and the easier it is to monitor them. That means sitting next to or near them at meals and in some group activities.

Also, get extra help if you can. A junior counselor or counselor-in-training (CIT) who can help you with the group can free you up to spend some extra time with a camper who needs it. The trick here is not to spend so much time with special needs that the needs of the entire group get sacrificed.

With some care, planning, and a thoughtful approach, counselors can have more success with "fast" kids in ways that help both them and the other children to thrive at camp.

Adults with ADHD

1. Some 70 % of children with ADD have some symptoms into adulthood.
2. Counselors with ADD best suited to specific jobs at camp—could run special activities or events.

Dear Bob,

How about a follow-up to your column on ADD/ADHD—one that deals with attention deficit disorder in staff. Some of the new information out on ADD in adults may have ramifications for working with staff as well as for directors. Learning about this new information opened my eyes to some of the coping mechanisms that might be helpful to others.

Lisa Durrell
Massachusetts

Dear Lisa,

Thank you for the opportunity to share some new information about ADD in adults. Since it is now understood that, with about 70 percent of children with ADD, some of their symptoms persist into adulthood, knowing some of the signs can help directors identify the syndrome in themselves and in staff and can help them develop creative ways of adapting to camp. After all, you can't remedy a challenging behavior unless you know it exists and how it impacts your work with others.

This statistic, which makes it clear that many children with ADD/ADHD become adults with symptoms of ADD/ADHD, contradicts the belief commonly held just a few years ago that children outgrow the disorder during puberty. Unfortunately, many adolescents who don't get help with their ADHD often engage in troublesome activities that are actually attempts to control the constant buzzing they experience in their heads. One such behavior is drug abuse, which for some youngsters with ADHD is an attempt to self-medicate. Another is engaging in high-risk behavior, which is a way ADHD kids calm the noise inside—they simply match it with adrenaline bursts from their high-risk activities.

I hear frequently directors ask, "What happened to ADHD folks before we knew about it?" One answer is that such people gravitated toward jobs or careers where their energy could be utilized constructively, such as on the frontier, in the circus or theater, in highly active jobs, and so on. There were more open spaces and more opportunities for hands-on work that could occupy some people with ADHD—either that or they ended up in jail. Indeed, many experts believe that the prison population in the United States has an inordinately high percentage of people with ADHD—people who simply could not make sense out of their world or whose risk-taking adaptations got them into trouble. Thom Hartmann, author of the book *Attention Deficit Disorder: A Different Perception* (Underwood-Miller, 1993), argues that ADD is really an adaptive trait and not a disorder. He suggests, for example, that adults with what is now called ADHD would have been the ones who did the hunting in premodern days. These are folks whose bursts of energy and propensity toward action would have made them well suited for hunting, while they would have been ill suited for and bored with the routines of farming, gathering, or living a more settled tribal life.

My experience with adults at camp who have had ADHD but who have not had it diagnosed is that they have been able to survive at camp by developing various coping mechanisms to compensate for their disability. One way counselors with ADHD might adapt at camp, assuming they are able to function reasonably well in the community, would be to run special activities or events—activities that require creativity, familiarity with chaos, and a lot of movement and excitement. It would be deadly for such people to have positions that required tracking a lot of mundane detail or being tied to a routine that does not change.

What are some signs to look for if you as an adult think you might have some form of ADD/ADHD? The following is a partial list of traits.

- Fails to finish projects/classes/assignments
- Acts before thinking
- Is always on the go
- Is sensitive to criticism
- Thinks negatively, even after an exciting or positive experience
- Has difficulty when reading
- Has difficulty being and staying organized
- Has trouble managing a checkbook
- Tends to be a poor planner
- Has trouble prioritizing
- Is outspoken and/or impatient with a group process
- Prefers to work solo as opposed to on a committee
- Has difficulty giving or receiving soothing and holding (except, perhaps, with children)
- Tends to be great at identifying children with ADHD

For more information on ADHD in adults, read *Attention Deficit Disorder in Adults* (Taylor, 1992) by Lynn Weiss. There is both a workbook and a text.

Tourette's Syndrome in Campers

1. TS symptoms:
   - motor tics
   - vocal tics
   - sometimes intense, sometimes disappear
   - change over time
   - low self-esteem and shame
   - short fuse
2. Many with TS have ADHD, too.

Dear Bob,

We have just discovered that we have enrolled a youngster with Tourette's Syndrome. Can you tell us a little about it, including what we can expect from this young fellow and what special challenges he might pose to our staff? Any ideas about where we can get information on the subject would also be helpful.

Concerned in California

Dear Concerned,

Tourette's Syndrome (often referred to as TS by educators and mental health workers) is an inherited neurobiological disorder that usually first appears in children in their early elementary school years. There are four characteristic features of TS, the most commonly observed of which is involuntary multiple motor tics—things like sudden jerking of the head or shoulders, rolling or blinking of the eyes, and tapping or repetitive touching.

The second feature is something called vocal tics. These involuntary noises can include throat clearing, growling, repeated coughing, or a variety of other sounds or utterances. Some children with TS display echolalia (repeating what others have just said), while others may blurt out socially inappropriate words (technically known as coprolalia). While very few children with TS actually manifest this last trait, it has become one of the most notorious traits associated with TS.

The third characteristic of TS is that there are times when the symptoms can be very intense and other times when the symptoms virtually disappear. It is also clear that, for short periods of time, some children with TS can, with extraordinary effort, suppress some of their behaviors for various amounts of time. Thus, a child with vocal tics might be able to be quiet during vespers or some other camp assembly, but will experience a greater intensity of tics back at the cabin at bedtime. This may at first appear manipulative on the part of some children, so it is best to educate staff about TS if they will have contact with such a child.

The fourth characteristic of TS is that symptoms may change over time. One year a child may exhibit eye blinks and head movements, while the next year he or she may display clicking noises with the tongue and shoulder shrugs.

The most severe consequence for children with TS may be low self-esteem due to shame they may feel about their behavior. Some children with TS have a short fuse and lose their tempers quickly. Others are sensitive to criticism and hold back from making friends. Although most cases of TS are mild, you should talk with the parents about their child (how the child has adjusted, what works, and so on), as well as with any physician who might be involved. Many children with TS are on medication to control the tics. The most common is Catapres, the same medication used in adults to control blood pressure. Catapres seems effective in only 50 percent of the cases. More recently pediatric neurologists have been using small doses of Risperdal with remarkable success.

Many children with TS also have ADHD, but, because of the underlying tic disorder, these children cannot take Ritalin. In this case the discussion needs to focus on how to help the child manage him- or herself in the social and learning settings at camp. Just as they do with other children with ADHD, camp directors need to establish with parents what the social skill level is of any TS child, with or without ADHD. This will help determine whether a child is ready for a social community like camp. You can find such a checklist in my recently published staff resource manual, *Lifelines and Safety Nets* (little fox productions, ltd., 1995). For more information on TS itself, contact

Tourette's Syndrome Association
42-40 Bell Boulevard, Suite 205
Bayside, New York 11361-2874
718/224-2999

Campers with Eating Disorders

1. Dealing with anorexia nervosa, bulimia—overeating and purging—and binge eating disorder.
2. Camp director responsibilities:
   - enlisting qualified medical assistance
   - establishing monitoring system
   - bringing parents into alliance with medical personnel

Dear Bob,

We are an all-girls camp in the South with adolescent campers who, in recent years, have been struggling more and more with eating disorders. One case last summer was particularly disturbing to us.

A fourteen-year-old camper I'll call Alice came to camp without any warning from her parents that she might be having a problem with her weight or with eating. Alice had been with us the previous year, so we were stunned to see how thin she had become. When we expressed our alarm to her parents, at first her mother flatly denied there was any problem. However, as conversations continued, she finally admitted that she "didn't want to make a big deal about it" and didn't want **us** to get into a struggle with Alice by talking about it with her directly. Our concern was Alice's ability to maintain her health in our rigorous, active camp program, especially in the summer heat. Against the protests of the parents, we put the girl on close monitoring and found she was eating very little. She did manage to eat just enough, thereby assuring that she could remain at camp for the summer. However, she did go home from camp weighing five pounds **less**. The parents' response? They were angry with us that we didn't let them know she was losing weight!

Bob, what can we do to protect ourselves and the campers, get through to the parents, and understand this problem better?

Worried, but Still Eating

Dear Eating,

When it comes to camp directors' concerns about campers, your letter speaks to one of four major issues most often mentioned in an informal survey I conducted last summer in the more than thirty-six camps I visited from May to August. (The other three are ADHD, increased aggressiveness and conflict among campers, and a surge in rudeness toward adults by all campers and by girls in particular.)

Your letter is also timely. In October 1995, the Carnegie Foundation published a study that voiced concern about the rise of serious signs of stress among girls in the United States, eating disorders being one of the

66

leading symptoms. Although this is a topic far more complicated than can be thoroughly addressed here, let me cover some main points.

Anorexia nervosa, bulimia, and binge eating disorder (BED) are the three eating disorders most familiar to the general public. Anorexia is characterized by weight loss ranging from minor to life threatening as the result of abstinence or minimal eating. Anorexia is the most serious of the three eating disorders in that it can result in death or long-term damage as a result of malnutrition. Children who suffer from anorexia tend to have a highly distorted image of their own bodies, can be perfectionistic, and are often involved in strenuous activities like gymnastics, ballet, intensive aerobics, running, or, for boys, wrestling. Demands of the activity often reinforce the belief of anorexics that they are fat or in need of further weight reduction. The female camper, Alice, in your letter sounds like she suffered from anorexia.

Bulimia is a condition whereby the person overeats and then induces vomiting or uses laxatives to purge herself of the excess calories. Bulimics cycle through periods where they engage in bingeing and purging only rarely to several times in one day. The most immediate concern from a physiological point of view is loss of energy and electrolytes, though bulimics also experience damage to their teeth, epiglottis, larynx, and so on from repeated vomiting.

Individuals with BED cycle between futile dieting attempts and uncontrolled eating binges similar to those of bulimia. Unlike bulimics, however, those with BED do not purge.

The underlying causes of eating disorders are varied and complicated. Suffice it to say that they include issues of control; a desire to separate and have greater autonomy, countered by a desire to remain connected; an attempt to adapt to past trauma; and a barometer of family stress. Girls are afflicted with eating disorders far more often than boys, although boys have recently been reported to be suffering from anorexia (especially runners and wrestlers) in greater numbers. It is only a matter of time until more camps begin seeing anorexic boys and male staff.

Some girls have described losing weight as the only thing they felt they had control over. Others have talked about feeling like they had to "mold myself to my mom and dad," by taking their parents' beliefs in, only to spit them out, literally, in an attempt to regain autonomy. Still others have talked about weight loss as a way of countering feelings of inadequacy and rejection, their bodies being the one thing they can do something about, thus recouping control and gaining a sense of mastery in a world in which they feel helpless.

The most important thing for camp directors to remember, however, is that it is not your job to analyze the cause of a camper's eating disorder. An eating disorder is a psychological problem that can have serious medical complications. It is your job to do the following:

1. Enlist qualified medical help in assessing whether the child can remain safely at camp.
2. Create a monitoring system, with the proper personnel involved, to assure the continued health of the child if she does remain at camp.
3. Create an alliance with the parents and the proper medical personnel aimed at ensuring the child's continued well-being (and reducing your exposure to risk in taking on the responsibility of having this child in camp).

Some people might wonder why we should even risk having such a child in camp. The truth is that most children with an eating disorder arrive at camp without directors having prior knowledge. Of all behavioral difficulties a child might have, this is one where the denial of the parents is often extremely high. Even when confronted by the facts, parents will continue to deny that there is a problem and in some cases will unwittingly contribute to it. In the case you describe, it sounds like Alice's parents did have some prior knowledge of her condition, but were hiding it from the camp, probably out of fear that you would not accept her or out of some magical thinking of their own that the problem would just disappear. In a case in California similar to the one you describe, the mother of a camper complained to the camp that she had not been told that her daughter had been losing weight at camp and then added how "great Samantha looks in the new clothes I bought her since she's been home."

Your strategy is to ask to speak to the child's pediatrician or the family doctor. If you make speaking to the family doctor a qualification for keeping the child at camp, you will get greater cooperation. Stick to your guns. No cooperation gives you nothing to work with and makes it too risky for you and the child to have her remain in your program.

The doctor may tell you something quite different from what a parent claims the doctor has said. Furthermore, if you have concerns about continued weight loss, have the doctor and the camp medical personnel work out arrangements for monitoring the child's health and weight that keep you and the child's counselors out of the struggle. Remember that this behavior is often a manifestation of some struggle between parent(s) and child for power, control, autonomy, and so on—one struggle you want to stay out of. You will have greater success establishing an alliance with a child if you let the medical folks do the job of weigh-ins and the like. Hovering over a child at meals or counting calories only gets you or your staff entangled in the problem. If a camp doctor or nurse, working with the family doctor, decides a child has fallen below the weight level established as the one she must maintain to stay at camp, then it frees you to remain supportive, concerned, and not a policing force. In other issues I often recommend that directors and staff take a direct, strong stand. With eating disorders, you must be shrewd in a different way or the child will only escalate her behavior (often putting stones in her pockets at weigh-ins or getting into other deceptive behavior at mealtime).

Another advantage of getting the medical folks to do their job is that it will free you from getting into a struggle with parents who are too frightened or who are otherwise invested in minimizing their child's problem, while giving you better coverage with regard to risk. Some children with eating disorders find camp to be a refuge—one that is less conflicted than their environment at home, which can help them refrain from their symptomatic behavior while they are at camp.

---

unit two
campers and staff

Your Biggest Kids—Your Greatest Resource

A camp's staff is its greatest resource. No matter how wonderful or well endowed its physical setting, a camp is not so much a place as it is people. Regardless of how rich or varied the program may be, it is only as strong as the people who bring it to life. In many ways, the staff members are the heart and soul of a camp, interpreting its philosophy and impacting campers through the relationships they form.

The other side of this coin is that counselors are also the biggest kids at camp. Every director knows intuitively that most people who end up at camp—who choose to be there—are kids at heart. Directors know this largely because it was once probably true of them at some point earlier in their own careers (and, in some cases, may still be true!).

Problems occur, however, when staff members regress, caving into their more childish instincts, making poor judgments, and setting poor examples. After all, one of the riskiest things young adults can do is put themselves in the presence of groups of children for long periods of time. This is because there are certain occupational hazards that come from working with children. One of them is the tendency to begin mirroring their impulsive, chaotic, reactive behaviors. When this happens, counselors can start to look and act just like campers. While being *childlike* can be an asset when working with children in that it helps in being able to relate to their world, being *childish* only means being a bigger kid than the kids themselves. Under these conditions staff can be a camp's single greatest liability. (My friends in insurance tell me it is the human factor that creates the greatest insurance risk.)

The technical term for this phenomenon is "regressive pull." Children do, in many ways, exert a kind of pull on adults to join them in their less-than-grown-up antics. Because children tend to be noisy, messy, impulsive, imperfect, dependent, and curious, working and living with them causes stress. If that stress is great, it can lead to a regression in any caretaker's behavior. Staff who are younger or less mature are especially susceptible to regressive pull because they are, developmentally, only a few steps ahead of the children in their care. They have fewer internal resources and strategies and less experience to ward off the regression.

While experience and the maturation process are the only true defenses against regressive pull, camp leaders can do more to raise the awareness level of staff and give them tools for working with children. Some of these practices include the following:

Role playing; challenging camper behavior. Done in small groups with facilitators who can set a serious tone and have real-life scenarios, this helps staff to "try on" new approaches.

Discussion groups. Focusing on typical camper situations, like homesickness or cleanup times, staff can share past experience and brainstorm what works. Reporting or summarizing results can reinforce the learning.

Initiatives. Specific task-focused group initiatives where participants are *properly debriefed* can help staff recognize their working style and observe or create new approaches to challenging situations.

Outside speakers. This can add depth and specific knowledge to orientation or ongoing training. Child therapists, social workers, special education teachers, and even parents can provide practical examples that staff can integrate into their repertoire.

Challenge course work. This, like initiatives, can help staff work together and raise awareness only if they are properly debriefed and then only if the course work is related to situations at camp.

Films or videos. Material on child behavior can add insight and develop a more aware way of thinking about group process, listening, redirecting behavior, and so on.

Parent panels. Made up of procamp, savvy parents, these panels can help counselors look at their work more seriously while gaining new strategies on handling certain child behaviors.

These are just a few ideas for enhancing camp-staff interactions through training opportunities. The subject matter comprising the second unit in this book on campers and staff presents other specific tools that counselors need in order to be more effective, thereby reducing the risk of being punitive with campers or overreacting with them. These include tips on handling homesickness and dealing with bullies and scapegoats, as well as other techniques such as giving choices, secret signals, redirecting, and smoothing.

Unit two also deals with the managerial relationships that camp leaders have with staff, such as supervising them and assessing grounds for dismissal, along with protocol for firing staff. Most camping professionals get little if any training in some of these areas. As caretakers, many directors hold onto staff longer then they probably should out of a desire to let the "magic" of camp turn this person around. When a staff person is let go, however, it is often done so poorly that it seriously injures the trust and morale of the rest of the staff.

The strategies and procedures in this unit were written with the goal of helping camp directors and staff to choose how they interact with campers and each other. That is, the techniques herein allow camping professionals to be more methodical, thoughtful, and deliberate in their work with staff instead of gut reacting or following an outmoded tradition, while helping staff be the same with campers. It is this spirit of aware and thoughtful action and response that helps create a safe environment—an envelope of safety—at camp for everyone who is part of its community.

Counselors Helping Campers

1. Counselors need to help kids get to know each other and to feel welcome.
2. Allow kids to be experts.
3. Listen.
4. Practice speaking.
5. Set clear limits.
6. Allow kids to save face.
7. Respond rather than react.

Dear Bob,

I am a counselor at a camp in New England, and I enjoy reading your column. I especially like the different things you say about making a difference with campers. Do you have any new ideas for a third-year counselor about working with campers?

Bound for Maine

Dear Bound,

Thank you for your letter. Here are a few things to keep in mind as you go through the summer.

1. Beginnings are crucial. Be present in the cabin or meeting area when campers arrive. Help them feel welcome. Facilitate their getting to know you and each other. Tip: Two things that make children feel left out at camp are not knowing the names of other campers and not knowing the words to songs.
2. Allow children to be experts. Many children come to camp with a lot of knowledge about hobbies, sports, and camp itself. Allowing campers to show off what they know helps them feel a sense of mastery and establishes mutual respect. Tip: Have returning campers show new campers around.
3. Take time to listen. Many children are not used to adults listening to them, so they will be impressed when you do. Feeling unheard or misunderstood makes kids stop listening to us.
4. Practice public speaking. You will undoubtedly have to address groups of people at camp, so practice speaking up clearly, making eye contact, getting to the point, and resisting the temptation to include "in" jokes that many won't understand.
5. Set clear limits. Know when to say "no." Setting limits means helping children take "no" for an answer. This may be difficult

for you if you have a hard time with children being temporarily angry at you. But when children *feel* out of control, they often *get* out of control, and that is when people get hurt (physically or emotionally). Being a counselor is not a popularity contest.

6. Allow children to save face. What children fear more than anything is being shamed. If you characteristically deal with children in a way that humiliates them, they will resent you and stop listening to you.

7. Notice whether you are *reacting* or *responding* to situations at camp. Reacting means being impulsive, not controlling your gut feelings, and not thinking of consequences. Responding means checking your impulses, stopping to think, and not letting your gut reactions dictate what you do and say. This useful self-check can be employed in your interactions with campers, fellow counselors, key staff, and directors.

There are many things to learn and know about working with children, but if you take the time to enter a child's world and play and have fun, you'll be engaging with them in a meaningful way. This seems to occur less and less in our society. Make sure camp is one place this can still happen.

Children Need a Firm but Patient Hand to Establish Self-Control

1. Campers need to be helped toward self-control.
2. Counselor-camper friendships ease way.
3. Counselor control also needed.

Dear Bob,

I would appreciate it if you could address the topic of children's abusive behavior toward other children—teasing, hazing, and so on—and the counselor's role as a preventative agent.

I believe counselors need to think about the importance of limit setting and its relationship to supervision, as well as how to maintain a supportive and nurturing role with campers.

Ray Kalman
Snow Mountain Camp
Nevada City, California

Dear Ray,

With camps across the country about to gear up for orientation, staff training, and the arrival of summer, your question is timely, indeed.

As anyone who has worked with them knows, children can be the most thoughtful, warmest people in the world. They can also be the cruelest. Ostracizing other children and being outwardly derisive, exclusive, or vindictive are all activities that youngsters are capable of engaging in from time to time.

When thinking about the behavior of children toward other children, we must keep two things in mind. First, children are in the process of growing up and do not come as ready-made adults. Second, children often reflect and act out the attitudes and behaviors of the adults whose company they keep. I would like to consider these factors one at a time.

One way I think about growing up is that it is the process of gaining better control over one's feelings and impulses. As camp professionals know, children do not always have good impulse control; that is, they don't have very good brakes. Once they get started, they have a very hard time stopping. If you have any doubts about this, watch a group of children in a friendly water-balloon fight and see what happens. Very often it degenerates into a free-for-all that gets increasingly difficult to manage without someone's feelings getting hurt.

Until children get better at controlling their feelings, they are often ruled by them. When they feel something, whether it's anger, jealousy, homesickness, or compassion, it is as if they *become* what they feel. Children are known for experiencing what they feel with abandon. Unfortunately, their capacity to stop and think, delay gratification, and express their feelings in ways that are not impulsive has not yet developed to a point where they can always be civilized.

Some examples: A child feels threatened by a new camper in her group, and, rather than seek reassurance from her counselor and friends, she gets the others to exclude the newcomer. One camper, under a lot of internal pressure to excel, teases a younger, less talented youngster when he messes up in an activity. Two boys playwrestling get overly aggressive, and, instead of backing off and admitting he is hurt, one boy gets angry and hits the other.

These are all examples of children who need a firm but patient hand in establishing better self-control. Left to their own devices, these youngsters might become abusive to the point of damaging someone emotionally, if not physically.

Enter staff, which is the second point I mentioned earlier. The first thing for staff to know is what I have just described—that children are by nature impulsive and need guidance and structure.

The second thing for counselors to remember is that children will be more likely to respond to staff if they have cultivated a friendship first. In fact, the single greatest defense against the appearance of abusive behavior in children is the presence of well-developed relationships with caring but firm adults. When these relationships are characterized by staff who listen to and acknowledge a child's experience and interests, they are even more effective. The counselor's job is to enter a child's world without becoming childish.

A third and very important point is that counselors need to be aware of their own tendencies to be teasing, abusive, or punitive, since children will emulate what staff members *do* rather than what they *say* children should do. Humiliating a child or barking orders at a child or fellow staff member does not create an environment of acceptance and emotional safety, free from hazing and abusive behavior. Nonverbal messages influence children to a far greater degree than verbal ones.

The exception, of course, is swearing. A lot could be said about swearing, but suffice it to say that swearing represents a momentary loss of impulse control. When adults exhibit this kind of behavior in front of children, not only are they suggesting that swearing is okay, they are also implying that a temporary loss of self-control doesn't matter. For children whose impulse control may be shaky to begin with and whose second greatest fear and single greatest temptation is loss of self-control, this is not a helpful message. While there are some specialized exceptions not relevant to this discussion, swearing does a lot to contribute to a potentially abusive environment.

A fourth factor for staff to fathom is that, as with most things, children get better at mastering their feelings through practice. With practice comes mistakes, and, while children need to be accountable for their actions, we need to be patient. Growing up takes time.

Put another way, camp provides a myriad of opportunities for children to get a better grip on their feelings and impulses, but they cannot do this without the presence of genuinely interested adults who can give them what they cannot give themselves.

children need a firm but patient hand to establish self-control

Counselor-Camper Interactions: Missing Home and Camper Crushes

1. Homesick campers
   - may create premature closeness with counselor
   - when they make friends with other campers, they pull away and renounce their over-dependence
2. Camper crushes on counselors (same sex)
   - hero worship

Dear Bob,

I was a counselor last summer at a large, all-girls camp that I liked a lot. Something happened, though, that I'm still a little upset about.

There was a girl in my cabin who was missing home the first week of camp. I ended up spending a lot of time with her and we became very close.

After about one week she began to make friends, which was great, but then she began to act as if I didn't exist. I was very hurt, but I don't think it was something I did. I tried talking with her about it, but she was silent. Camp ended on a good note, but I'm still confused about what happened.

Melanie

Dear Melanie,

What you have described is a fairly common phenomenon. It seems that very homesick campers are forced into a kind of premature closeness by their needs. These youngsters demand a lot of time, energy, and reassurance from staff.

Once your friend made an adjustment to camp, however, her needs changed. Her crisis being over, she needed to catch up and join her peer group if she was to continue to fit in at camp.

Most children in this situation pull away, just like your friend did, in order to join with their peers and establish less dependent relationships—ones that renounce their overdependence and build a more self-confident, self-reliant sense of self through a slower-paced, getting-to-know-you process of making friends.

The trouble is that, if you don't know what's happening, it can lead to a sense of loss and bewilderment. I suspect that, if you had known to *expect* that, once your young friend recovered from homesickness, she would *necessarily* do what she did, you would have seen it as a normal part of her growth at camp.

From the sound of how things turned out, however, it seems you not only didn't do anything wrong, but that you did a lot of things right. Perhaps the next time it won't cause such wear and tear on your feelings.

Dear Bob,

I am nineteen years old and was a first-year counselor at a boys' camp last summer. I worked mostly with the older boys, and it was a lot of fun. One thirteen-year-old (I'll call him Dave) seemed to like me a lot. He often sought me out just to talk and would stay after the other boys had left, just to hang out. A couple of kids once joked about him having a crush on me, I guess because of how much time we spent together, but it was in good fun and no one seemed to think much about it.

Once, however, on an overnight, he and I were hiking behind the rest of the group talking and he took my hand to hold. It surprised me and made me uncomfortable. I kind of barked at him that "guys don't do that!" It sort of scared me, because maybe he did have a crush on me, but I hope I didn't encourage him by being nice, or something like that. I think I hurt his feelings, but I'm not gay and I didn't know what else to do or say.

Tim

Dear Tim,

Thank you for having the courage to write about such a sensitive topic. Your letter provides an opportunity to talk about adolescent boys in a way that I think will help you understand what happened with your friend Dave.

Boys differ markedly from girls in the way they progress through their social and sexual development. Girls seem more likely to be interested in the opposite sex, even innocently and from an early age, while boys often go through a preliminary stage of hero worship before they discover girls. Boys need to strengthen their sense of themselves as male by admiring and emulating idealized male role models.

For boys who are hungry for male attention, the positive relationship with, for example, a responsive, caring, accepting camp counselor can generate strong feelings—ones that frighten some boys because they fear what these feelings might mean (e.g., "Does this mean I'm weak? A baby? Gay?"). The truth is that, 90 percent of the time, an early-adolescent crush on an older male hero is nothing more than the expression of innocent, nonsexual, but affectionate feelings that are well within normal developmental limits.

Thus, Dave's wanting to hold your hand conveyed quite normal, probably nonsexual feelings. It was how he chose to express his feelings that was unusual. Chances are that he is either younger emotionally than his peers or that he has such strong needs for affection, attention, and nurturing that he acted impulsively.

So what does one do in a situation like this? First, don't panic. While I can certainly understand your surprise and the awkwardness of the moment, had you known more about adolescent male crushes, I suspect it would have been less startling for you.

Second, simply accept his feelings by saying, "I know you like me, Dave," and validate them with "I like you, too, you know that." Then set a gentle limit— "But I think there are better ways for us to show that we like each other," or even, "but we don't need to hold hands to show that we like each other." You would handle the situation the same way even if Dave were gay, because the issue is not his sexuality, but the way you show that you care about each other.

Teaching Staff to be Authorities on Children

> 1. Younger staff concern to control the kids often stems from having poor self-control.
> 2. Level of moral reasoning varies for different ages. How well campers listen to adults depends on their level.
> 3. Counselors and campers need to develop listening skills.
> 4. Eight additional counselor skills to practice.

Dear Bob,

During staff orientation we often get a lot of questions, especially from younger or less experienced staff, about how to control campers. While we have answers of our own, we were wondering what else you might say to staff when they ask, "Why would a kid listen to me?"

Pensive in Pennsylvania

Dear Pensive,

Many counselors are concerned with the need to control campers. For some, the concern has to do with feeling they don't have the tools or the wherewithal to be effective with children. (Of course, we all feel that way at times.)

While some children defy limit setting and other attempts to help them develop better self-control, the intensity with which some staff focus on control says more about them than it does about campers. It is as if they imagine campers are going to behave in ways that they themselves sometimes feel tempted to behave (e.g., impulsive, rebellious, defiant).

The obsession many younger staff have with controlling the kids stems, in part, from the anxiety they have about their own shaky internal policeman. This anxiety often masquerades as an urgent need for ways to control campers. As a young staff member at a midwestern camp once said to me in a moment of humorous revelation, "If the kids are out of control, well, gee, it might get contagious!" And it usually does!

Indeed, have you ever witnessed a showdown between a stubborn or defiant youngster and a threatened but aggressive younger staff member? Before long, you can't tell the camper from the staff.

Do such staff members need to be weeded out or considered unhealthy members of the community? I think not. Most young adults have unresolved issues about self-control and authority and experience

83

some anxiety when they anticipate spending a lot of time being exposed to the demands of children (who are, by nature, easily stimulated, noisy, impulsive, messy, and imperfect).

It is reassuring to staff to learn the definition of the word "authority," which comes from the root, "author." To have enough knowledge, expertise, and skill to be able to author something (like a play or a lesson or a code of conduct in a cabin) and therefore to be an authority on the matter is different from having a license to boss people around. Thus, to be able to respond to children effectively, counselors need to be good authors of words and deeds.

Staff also need to know that most children *want* to behave. They want the summer to go well; they want to like their counselors and they are, therefore, eager to please and cooperate to have fun.

Children want to listen to grown-ups for different reasons depending on their stage or level of moral reasoning. This is important because it means that counselors need to use different strategies with children operating at different stages of moral reasoning. For camp-age children, the levels and ages to which they *roughly* correspond are as follows:

1. **Reasoning:** "I listen because I want to stay out of trouble." Typical of the four- to six-year-old set; these children are most compliant and eager to please.
   What works best: Strong, friendly presence of adults; simple, clear, and specific consequences; measured but *immediate* feedback; time-outs; quiet firmness. Counselors who engage in fantasy play with children and stand up to their demands for attention will do well.

2. **Reasoning:** "I'll go along with this if there's something in it for me!" Usually five- to eight-year-olds think this way.
   What works best: Praise; giving responsibility; giving status by awarding favors, approval, and the like; time-outs; allowing children to earn their way back into good graces through specific tasks.

3. **Reasoning:** "I'll listen to my counselor if she is nice to me." What constitutes being nice includes fairness; showing interest; allowing a child to be the expert, encouraging and supporting competence and mastery; giving credit; listening. Ages eight to twelve or fourteen.

4. **Reasoning:** "I'll listen to my counselor if the group I hang with think she's nice." Age fourteen and older.
   The same things that make a counselor nice to an individual are ones that make him or her acceptable to the group, with one important addition: not making a big deal out of an adolescent's feelings while in the presence of peers.

As always, counselors need help developing their listening skills, no matter what the age of campers with whom they are working. It is their anxiety about control that pushes counselors to *act* rather than just listening first.

Counselors need to practice such things as being on the same physical level with younger children, taking campers aside, making eye contact, getting rid of distractions, acknowledging feelings, giving credit, inviting reflection, and sharing their own experiences with older campers. These skills will create an atmosphere that encourages children to listen to them. With careful discussion, exercises, and patience during staff training and ongoing support during the camp season, the staff can become any camp's most important and influential resource.

Staff Training Tips

1. Staff are a camp's single greatest resource.
2. Icebreakers and fun exercises allow staff to get to know each other, and provide a repertoire they can use with campers.
3. Role playing to learn new skills—six guidelines.
4. Remedies for three common mistakes staff often make with campers
   - state what you want campers to do
   - tug-of-war trap
   - listen for feelings

As the summer approaches and directors begin to think about staff orientation and training, I would like to share some of the tips and insights I gathered from my work with camps around the country during the past year.

The essential thing to remember about staff is that they are a camp's single greatest resource. Whatever your program, philosophy, or belief about children, your success will only be as great as your staff is strong, committed, and on board. Unless you have taken steps to develop trust with your staff, to make them feel a part of the planning and the program, and to give them opportunities to learn and practice skills, you may find that your camp is not as able to give kids a world of good as you might want.

Let me share with you two activities that counselors have identified as most valuable to them during orientation. Based on responses to an informal survey I conducted during the summer of 1995 in which about 2,000 counselors participated, the first item that counselors said was most helpful to them were the icebreakers and exercises that were fun, allowed them to get to know one another, and gave them a kind of repertoire to use with the campers. In other words, the thing that promoted trust, teamwork, and a greater sense of family was the opportunity to socialize in a constructive, planned way through the use of activities. As long as these activities are inclusive, promote teamwork (in other words, minimize or *contain* competition), and are fun, they keep staff morale high, create a better attitude toward sessions that require sitting and listening, and prepare the staff for the second item they said was most useful to them during orientation—role-playing true-to-life-at-camp scenarios involving campers or other staff.

Role playing is a highly effective way to teach skills. It allows staff to see in advance the kinds of challenges campers will present them with before it actually happens, thus avoiding the shock that often hits new or foreign counselors as the summer unfolds. Role playing also helps staff develop a sense of readiness by giving them an opportunity to practice skills that may be new, unfamiliar, or even counterintuitive to them. Spending time on this kind of endeavor may be the most valuable thing you do with your staff, but it can be undertaken successfully only if the proper guidelines are followed. The following are the kinds of things you will need to keep in mind.

1. Role playing means exposing yourself in front of other staff. In order for this to happen, there needs to be enough trust present or people will not feel comfortable enough to take the risk. Use icebreakers, team-building activities, and other opportunities for staff to get to know and work with one another to establish a culture that allows for trial and error. Get staff to talk about relevant issues in a serious way in small groups before launching into role playing.

2. Get your key staff to plan ahead, developing a list of scenes for role playing that are from the actual history of the camp. Doing this will give your key staff a stake in the endeavor and will also convey to new staff what kinds of challenges they can expect from campers.

3. Get old-timers involved in the process. You can do this by holding a mini-precamp conference some weekend day or evening with your veterans going over some of the role-play material and gathering additional scenarios. In addition to making them feel included in the process, it is a good way to encourage returning staff to share their ideas with new staff once orientation is under way.

4. During the role-playing sessions, which should be done in small groups for better results, constantly reiterate some of your values. These can include, but are not limited to, such things as *being nonjudgmental* when people are learning; living out the tenet that it is *okay to be a novice* (that people will not laugh at or criticize you but will support you as you go through the process of trial and error); demonstrating that, *at camp, we are all learners.* If your staff can truly embrace this concept, you will already have gone a long way toward providing an emotionally safe place for campers to try out new things.

5. During the role-playing sessions, weave in the skills you want your staff to practice. I'll discuss this later.

During the role-playing sessions, point out the three mistakes most people who work with children seem to make repeatedly. The first mistake is that most people are more likely to tell children what they don't want them to do, rather than what they do want them to do. For example, we will often say to children, "Don't fight!" "Stop running!" "Quit arguing!" "Leave him alone!" The problem with this is that children have a much better idea of what we *don't* want them to do than of what we *do* want them to do. No wonder many child-care folks become exasperated with how children behave! It takes awareness and a concerted effort to break this old, overlearned habit, but stating things in positive terms—what we *want* from children—pays dividends.

The second common mistake people make with children is falling into what I call the tug-of-war trap. Suppose, for example, a child says, "I'm not making my bed! My parent(s) didn't pay money for me to come to camp to work, I came to have fun!" Most unseasoned counselors fall for the bait and immediately get caught in an argument about who paid what for camp and whether a child must make his or her bed. Mostly this happens because counselors don't know what else to do, which is why you need to introduce alternatives.

The third most common mistake people make with children is to miss the *feeling tone* of what children are saying. In other words, we become fixated on behavior and miss that a child may be acting out of fear, sadness, or a sense of loneliness. Unless counselors are trained to identify and name feelings, much of what campers communicate to them may get lost.

As with all training, helping staff learn more effective ways of being with children is a process that needs to continue—with follow-up, retraining, and new (live) examples—throughout the summer. If directors and camp administrators make time for this kind of ongoing training, they can expect to deliver the caliber of child care for which they might want to have a reputation with parents—one that truly gives kids a world of good.

88

Providing Counselors with Skills

> 1. Counselors need effective communication tools.
> 2. Brainstorm with group about "rules."
> 3. Help each camper make one new friend.
> 4. Responses to resistant camper behavior
>   - give choices
>   - this for that
>   - smoothing
>   - state expectation, disengage

Dear Bob,

Every year I have young adults join our staff who start out the season with great enthusiasm, only to be stymied when it comes to managing camper behavior. What many of our staff need are more ways to work successfully with campers when they won't make their beds, brush their teeth, clean up, or go to activities. Can you help?

Marty Griffin
Saddle Rock Camp for Girls
Mentone, Alabama

Dear Marty,

You are raising a question that I believe both is at the heart of counselor burnout and has the potential to make counselors be mean or inappropriate with campers—the lack of effective tools.

When a counselor is confronted by a resistant camper, he or she often experiences a sense of shock, frustration, and powerlessness. If we could listen to the dialogue inside the counselor's mind at such a juncture, we might hear things like, "What do you *mean*, you won't listen to me? What will I look like if I can't get you to do what I am supposed to do? I'll look foolish and incompetent! This is not what I bargained for!"

When counselors, be it at day or residential camp, lack simple, useful ways of responding to resistant campers (or any challenging camper behavior, for that matter), they usually have one of two reactions—fight or flight. In the fight mode, counselors are likely to escalate into a power struggle with campers, thereby raising the risk of mistreating or physically abusing the camper or breaching the envelope of safety most camps try to establish for campers. In the flight response, counselors, out of their fear of appearing inept and feeling helpless, begin to withdraw or distance themselves from campers. They can become apathetic, mildly depressed, or highly involved in activities that distract them from their life with campers, like drinking off duty, staying out late, oversleeping, and so on.

89

Obviously, the best first line of defense against camper misbehavior is for counselors to establish a strong, positive relationship with their campers. Counselors need to take time to enter their campers' world and find out what their interests are, what brought them to camp, and what they most look forward to doing at camp, for example. Since camp-age children are highly social, and since success with their peer group is important, help members of the group to get to know one another. Facilitate a meeting early in the session where the group members brainstorm together what "agreements" and "understandings" (better words than "rules") they have both about their responsibilities (cleanup, for example) and their treatment of each other. Finally, but perhaps the most important, help each camper make at least one new friend at camp. If you can do this you will have great success with your campers. That being said, what about resistant camper behavior? Here are four different responses you can use.

1. **Give choices**
   When to use: camper is not doing what is expected.
   Age group: all, depending on choices given or situation.
   Examples: Counselor: "You can either make your bed alone, or I can help you." Camper: "But I don't want to make my bed at all!" Counselor: "That isn't one of the choices. Let me tell you again what the choices are."

2 **This for that (positive consequences)**
   When to use: camper is not doing what is expected.
   Age group: lower or middle camp.
   Examples: "If you can help the group clean up, we can all play cards at rest hour." "If you help Doreen sweep, I'll help you with your bed." "If you can be done in three minutes, we can play ball later."

3. **Smoothing**
   When to use: uncooperative campers with little time to respond.
   Age group: lower and middle camp or teens in a regressed mood.
   Examples: "Look, I know we are all tired, but let's get through this last five minutes." "I know this is a drag, but, if we can tough this out for the next mile, we'll be there!"

4. **Redirecting behavior**
   When to use: campers who are beginning to tease or fight with one another.
   Objective: To divert campers into a more acceptable activity that absorbs or "redirects" their energy.
   Age group: with any age group if used with age-appropriate activities.

Examples: (younger children): "Hey, kids, let's all play 'follow the leader.'"
  (preteens): "Who wants to make a tent?"
  (teens): "I'm challenging you guys to a game of 21 on the basketball court!"

5. **State your expectation, disengage**
  When to use: camper(s) breaking or threatening to break rule/agreement.
  Age group: especially effective with teens, preteens.
  Example: "You are expected to go to swimming, so I will see you there in five minutes." Then avoid any further discussion and go about your business. Pattern to follow:
  1. State the expectation.
  2. Stay out of any arguments.
  3. Restate your expectation.
  4. Disengage.
  It works 90% of the time!

As with all interactions with campers, it is important for staff to remember the following:

Practice makes perfect. To be successful with any of these techniques, you need to role-play and try them out.

One size does not fit all. One technique may work with some campers and not others.

Don't take things personally. That doesn't mean you won't have feelings about defiant campers; it means you should remember not to seek revenge if your feelings are hurt.

You are not alone. Ask for help from cocounselors, unit directors, and others.

Listen. Defiant campers may be upset about something that may not be apparent. If you can get them to confide in you, you may discover what is really bothering them and dramatically change their attitude.

Keep your sense of humor. (Just take care not to use humor as a weapon.)

Growing up takes time. Remember, growing up doesn't happen as one smooth progression. Some of the most valuable camp experiences for children come from growing-up opportunities played out with staff. It is all part of a meaningful summer experience.

When Campers Ask about Sex

1. Discuss appropriate responses during staff orientation.
2. Acknowledge campers' curiosity as natural.
3. Let campers talk, but provide structure and containment.

The following letter is actually a composite of a number of inquiries I have received from staff members at many different camps. It represents what is clearly a delicate and difficult situation for many counselors.

Dear Bob,

As a counselor at an overnight camp, I have been caught in an awkward position with older campers that I know other counselors have experienced. I wonder if you have any ideas about what would help.

Sometimes, especially on overnights, campers will ask me about my personal experiences—not just about dating, but about what I do, if anything, in a romantic way on those dates. If I say nothing, campers feel offended and hurt, as if I am perhaps not as close to or as trusting of them as I say I am. Yet I am not sure it is such a good thing to be sharing my own personal experiences with campers about such a private matter. Finding the right words when you are on the spot isn't always easy.

Perplexed Counselor

Dear Perplexed,

Finding the words is, indeed, hard when you are in a close relationship with curious campers. One of the issues here is that this kind of problem needs to be talked about among staff during orientation before the campers arrive, since most counselors will encounter some version of your dilemma.

You are also correct to assume that "sharing [your] own personal experiences about such a private matter" is not always in the best interest of campers. First, many campers, while naturally curious, often get overstimulated when they hear about the private romantic lives of counselors. Not only can it make them silly or excited at that moment, but it can extend into other times when they may be tempted to do things they are not emotionally ready to handle.

The other concern is that we do not always know what a camper's prior experience might be, so we can never be sure what something we say to a camper might *mean* to him or her. Something we might say to campers who have had a negative experience may be more upsetting to them than is apparent at the time.

I think the most important factor, however, is that curious campers are often more interested in what's on *their* minds than they are in what you have been doing on your dates. Campers who are thinking about sexual issues are usually trying to figure something out for themselves, which gives you the key as to how to respond to them.

My first suggestion is to *acknowledge that they are curious* and to say that you don't mind them being curious. Being curious is natural, so it is natural that they might ask you.

Quickly add that you think, however, that they are probably trying to figure something out for themselves; then ask them what that might be. It is far better to *let them talk* about what's on their minds than it is for you to talk about your personal exploits. If they are insistent on you telling them, mention that the truth is that everyone they ask will tell them something different, so that what you have or haven't experienced yourself is not as important as them figuring things out for themselves. You can help them much more by *listening* than you can by telling them about your own personal life.

One thing you might say to an overly inquisitive camper is something like, "You know, Kevin, when you care about someone you don't go telling other people what you do with them in private." If, while they are talking, the conversation does become too stimulating for them and they get silly, too boisterous, or too graphic in their conversation, you need to point that out and settle them down, perhaps by saying that continuing the discussion can occur only if they can control themselves.

It is important to recognize that, when we allow campers of any age to become too stimulated, we are doing them a disservice and allowing their environment to become less safe in an emotional way.

93

Counselors Helping Campers (Revisited)

1. Avoiding daughter's tantrums at having to share mother with others
   - assure that you like others but love only her
   - have a secret sign
   - establish reward system to lessen tantrums

Dear Bob,

I have a seven-year-old daughter who is a Brownie Girl Scout in a group that I lead. We both enjoy this, but lately, near the end of our meetings, my daughter has been having tantrums. They began as short-lived, mild episodes, but have escalated.

I have sensed this has something to do with her having to share me with six other little girls, but I have spoken with her and it has not helped. She knows that when I am in the group I must be the Brownie leader first and her mother second.

I am especially concerned about this because we are planning to go to a local Girl Scout camp this summer where I will be a volunteer. I was hoping to get some help resolving her outbursts before camp.

Panic in Detroit

Dear Panic,

You were on the right track when you said your daughter's behavior has something to do with her having to share you. But you got derailed when you said that, in the group, you are the Brownie leader first and her mother second. From your daughter's point of view, you are always her mother first! The tantrums are most likely her way of expressing her hurt and anger.

Acknowledge to her that she is right—you are her mother first. But explain that, while she has to share you with the other girls, she is your special Brownie. You might even refer to a special secret you and she have. Indeed, you *like* all the other Brownies, but you *love* only her.

You will also need to establish with your daughter some sort of secret sign for the Brownie meetings, like a wink of an eye or a thumbs-up. Tell her the sign is your way of signaling to her what a good job you think she is doing during the meeting. You will find that she will seek out your approval a lot at first and less often as she trusts that you will remember and respond with the sign she is looking for.

Next, establish a simple reward system with her to help diminish and finally extinguish the tantrums. Tell her that, if she can go for five meetings with no tantrums, she will earn a special prize. (The prize might be something like a trip to the movies or a goldfish.) Remember that children, like adults, operate on a trial-and-error basis, so you will need to give her little chances to make mistakes.

When she is doing well during a meeting and you catch her at it by, for example, winking your eye, you will find it will provide the boost of pride in herself she needs to continue.

Before camp, you might want to repeat your conversation about her being special and your need for her cooperation. During the camp the wink can simply stand for "I love you and I'm proud of you!"

unit three
managing staff

The Challenges of Staff

There is probably no business in which the owners and directors work as hard as camping professionals do all year, only to turn the entire operation over to a bunch of eighteen to twenty-two year olds for the crucial part of their year. That is what camping people do when they bring on their staff. For most camps, the bulk of staff come from college-age young adults, who are relatively inexperienced and unskilled at working with children. What is ironic about this arrangement is that the staff of any camp is probably its greatest single resource. A staff interprets a camp's philosophy, executes the program, and has the close contact with campers that makes or breaks the camping experience.

Given their tremendous responsibility, it is extremely important to give counselors the tools, the skills, and support they need to execute their job. Unfortunately, many camp operators make no distinction between staff orientation and training, and, in fact, use the two terms interchangeably. "Training" refers to acquiring and practicing a set of skills until a certain level of proficiency is reached. In the few short days before campers arrive—during what most people call staff orientation—this kind of practice cannot occur. What does occur then is that the staff gets oriented to the methods and procedures of the camp and the individuals of the staff begin to function as a team. Staff training does not occur until the children arrive. In a way, it is the campers who train the staff. The problem with this kind of on-the-job training is that mistakes count. Unlike other nonseasonal businesses, camps have only a few short weeks to get their entire operation right.

Working with the staff effectively requires a comprehensive approach that begins with the screening and interviewing process, progresses through the orientation period, includes ongoing support and training, and concludes with a final assessment and exit interview. Along the way, camp directors will need to deal with staff morale, creating a culture of honesty and integrity, and establish protocols for supervision and feedback and procedures for evaluating and firing staff. These are complicated issues that effect the level of care that staff members are able to provide campers. We'll look at some of these issues in this unit.

There are two complaints that staff commonly mention to me. The first of these is coming to camp and being surprised about the specific duties for which they are responsible. While it is true that some young adults are naive about responsibilities and commitment, it is also true that during the interview directors and operators as a whole could do a better job of describing the specific duties each staff member will be expected to perform.

Giving prospective staff information about their job at camp is one of several important goals of a solid interview. A carefully crafted interview accomplishes the following:

- assessing the candidate's experience working with children as separate and distinct from his or her experience in a skill or activity area
- noting a candidate's background in camping or other child care, educational, or experiential settings with children
- detailing a candidate's specific accomplishments or proficiencies in an activity area
- giving the candidate a clear picture of caretaking responsibilities with children and responsibilities in an activity area and giving a sense of what life at camp is like, including stressors, demands, and free time
- evaluating whether the candidate would be a good match for the camp in terms of camp philosophy, camper clientele, and the staff team assembled thus far
- doing rudimentary screening for potential child abuse, flexibility with children, and the ability to maintain good boundaries with children
- laying the groundwork for setting individualized goals for each staff member

As camping professionals realize the importance of assembling a quality staff, and as the needs of the children attending camp have increased, more and more directors have taken steps to ratchet up their skill levels in staff interviewing and screening. What is crucial from the staff's point of view is giving them a clear picture of what they can expect about life and responsibilities at camp.

The other complaint that I hear from staff members on a regular basis is the lack of clear, positive feedback and appreciation for all the hard work they do during the summer. What staff people often say is they hear all of what they do wrong and nothing of what they do right. The truth is that giving clear and specific feedback to staff is a tedious and difficult task. The best approach to this is management by walking around (MBWA). MBWA means getting out of the office and making a habit of walking through camp to observe what is going on. I find that the kind of feedback that does not seem to carry much weight with staff is when a director or owner gathers the staff together in one large group and gives a general compliment about how great the summer is going and what a great job everyone is doing. While this is nice and can set a positive tone, it is neither specific enough nor personal enough for staff to appreciate. Remember that, for better or worse, most young adults still take their job performance quite personally. The bad news is that giving negative feedback can sometimes lead to hurt feelings. However, the good news is that giving personal, specific, and immediate feedback can powerfully reinforce and sustain a counselor's performance throughout the summer. This can only be achieved through MBWA because it requires witnessing the interactions between staff and campers.

Likewise, giving negative feedback can be crucial to setting expectations and sustaining high standards of performance. I find that when directors or supervisors are direct, specific, brief, and timely in delivering negative feedback, the chances of it being received favorably are enhanced. Two phrases that I find useful when delivering such feedback are, "I'm uncomfortable with . . ." and "I'm having a hard time with . . . ." Using these phrases provides a way to break the ice while taking the edge off the negative criticism for the staff member involved. One practice I definitely do *not* recommend is that of giving someone a compliment, then stating the negative feedback, then finishing with a compliment. First, a lot of staff believe this to be disingenuous. Second, the positive feedback is tarnished because it is immediately undone by the negative feedback. Furthermore, the negative feedback can get lost in or diluted by the other information, which does not accomplish what directors want—to pinpoint and change undesirable staff behavior.

The other practice that seems to be very supportive of staff is continuing training throughout the summer. Ongoing training is most effective when conducted in small groups, assembled according to camper age group, and when specific examples of camper behavior and successful interventions can be discussed. Unfortunately, what most camps do is have full staff meetings—late in the evening when the staff is tired—focusing on logistics and general topics. While such meetings may be useful, they should not be confused with ongoing training and support. Staff training means revisiting some of the themes, techniques, and tools that have been introduced during orientation and applying them to specific cases with specific campers. For instance, you might discuss with a small group of counselors homesickness in younger campers. You might discuss a bed-wetting problem or how to ease a bunk or camper group in which the youngsters are at odds with one another. This kind of specific, situational approach is much more useful and meaningful to staff, who often have a sense of urgency about dealing with challenging camper behavior.

Remember that when faced with an uncertain situation regarding campers, most counselors fall back on the child-rearing techniques of their parents or schools. Part of the reason for this is that under stress, people tend to rely on what's familiar rather than risk embarrassment by trying something new that they have not yet mastered. That is why ongoing staff training is important. To develop and reinforce new behaviors and techniques and ways of responding to children you must help counselors overcome the tendencies to fall back on familiar, often inappropriate techniques, such as shaming, yelling, taking things away, or making other punitive responses. The more staff are threatened by challenging camper behavior and the less supported they are, the more they will tend to employ punitive power tactics as a desperate attempt to regain their sense of authority. Ongoing staff training and supervision can help reduce this tendency and lead to happier camper-counselor relationships.

Supervising staff is important if you are going to maintain quality control. I find that staff need very specific, almost visual descriptions of what you expect. A useful approach is that of making a checklist of *specific* behaviors you would like to see counselors be able to perform. Instead of "spending more time with the kids," you would list specific activities with kids, such as "sitting with them during lunch" or "playing quiet games with them during rest hour." The more specific you can be about the exact behaviors you are looking for, the better your chances of getting your staff to understand and comply. A checklist also gives you a frame of reference for measuring performance. You will have stronger grounds for dismissing staff who do not perform according to your expectations if you can document that you have given them specific, clear, and immediate feedback over time.

Dealing with staff is crucial to the overall spirit at camp. After all, staff people, most of whom have not yet been parents themselves, sacrifice a great deal to be with children in the intense ways that happen at camp. It is important that you realize that while staff can be your biggest kids, they clearly are your greatest resource. Maintaining morale and making reasonable responses to the needs staff have will make for an overall happier and safer camp community.

Trust and Communication with Staff

1. Is a go-between (designated listener) needed for staff and directors?
2. Staff fear retaliations.
3. Even if they are friendly, directors are authority figures and leaders of staff.
4. Directors should actively solicit feedback from staff.

Dear Bob,

As a new camp director, I recently attended a workshop on staff issues. I heard how some staff do not feel comfortable, for whatever reason, speaking to directors about certain important matters, and that many directors have someone on their team who serves as a go-between for them and the staff.

I have a hard time with this practice. Doesn't it seem that, if a director develops enough trust with staff, she could expect the staff to be honest and direct with her?

Wet behind the Ears

Dear Ears,

Obtaining honest feedback from staff is a chronic dilemma for directors. The problem is rooted in the very nature of the counselor-director relationship. First, a director is, besides everything else, the boss. Many staff members have difficulty telling directors about their mistakes or voicing disagreement for fear of retaliation.

I've learned from conversations with counselors that the retaliation they fear can take a number of forms—being regarded as incompetent; being disapproved of or rejected personally; losing status or feeling excluded; being fired.

The second problem is that, no matter how approachable directors may be, they are still authority figures. A number of counselors come to camp with unresolved authority issues that often get played out, usually unconsciously, with the director. Some counselors get into trouble in ways that they would no sooner discuss with a director than with their own parents.

The problems that constricted feedback can pose are obvious. If counselors are doing anything that might seriously affect their judgment or performance at camp, the emotional or physical safety of campers and others might be at stake.

I do agree with you that there is a lot a director can do to establish a climate of trust, mutual respect, and openness with staff. In addition, directors need to do more to actively solicit feedback from staff. Experience has shown this needs to be done from the start of orientation.

There are a variety of ways a director can go about soliciting feedback from staff. One is to reserve a portion of staff meetings for discussing reactions to policy, programs, and the like. Another is to develop a feedback sheet. If you use a feedback sheet with staff, follow these five simple guidelines.

1. Keep it simple
2. Keep it confidential—making names optional may net you more.
3. Use it early in the orientation program.
4. Respond to it—listen and let people know you have heard them.
5. Repeat its use.

Even if you take steps to develop better trust between you and your staff, you will find that there are times when some counselors won't communicate with you when perhaps they should. This is why directors have someone on staff who serves as their eyes and ears—someone whom counselors trust as much as directors do. To be certain, this is a relationship that can be abused. However, my experience is that most counselors know that, if they tell this designated listener the truth, it will make its way back to the director. As for directors, most have told me they feel better knowing someone on their team can provide perspective when needed.

103

Encouraging Growth

1. Staff going from being camper to first-year staff not expecting how hard it is.
2. Older staff can help relate:
   - how much work is involved
   - how to deal with friends who are still campers and older campers who will not listen to younger counselors

Dear Bob,

My husband and I operate a coed camp in the Midwest. We are very proud of the fact that a lot of our staff were once campers at our camp. We have what we think is a very fine counselor-in-training program.

One problem occurs year after year when a young adult goes from being a camper to being a counselor. No matter what we say or how we try to prepare him or her, it always seems like such a shock. Some of these first-year counselors never realized how much work it is to be a staff member, and they have a hard time not being on the receiving end of what happens at camp. Many older campers idealize the role of the counselor. When they think about becoming a counselor they tend to focus only on what they think are increased privileges. They can't appreciate or comprehend the amount of work that goes into the job.

I realize there may be no easy answer, but is there anything we can do short of living through it year after year?

Mrs. Midwest

Dear Mrs. Midwest,

There are a lot of difficulties associated with the transition between being a camper and being a counselor at camp. However, I do have one suggestion that you might find useful.

At some point during orientation, gather your first-year counselors together who have been at camp as campers, and have other staff members who have themselves been through that transition speak to the group. Have your experienced staff members speak as specifically and personally as possible about all the things they went through—the realization of how much work was required; the problem of dealing with friends who were still campers; the problem of older campers not wanting to listen to young counselors—whatever they may have faced when they first became members of the staff.

Since these staff members can speak from experience and are probably closer in age to first-year staff members than you and your husband, the credibility they have with the younger group is much greater than anyone else in camp. Though this orientation will not eliminate the struggle of first-year counselors, I think you will find it will help. You might even want to schedule one or two follow-up meetings after camp has started. It can be very powerful and validating for the young counselors to share with and learn from staff who have been in the same position.

Staff Motivation

1. Be clear about expectations and demands of job in interview.
2. Listen to staff experiences.
3. Allow staff to be experts.
4. Support staff's efforts with kids.
5. Feedback needs to be specific and individualized.

Dear Bob,

You have spoken about staff training, but my question is about motivation. Every year we have a few staff members who never quite catch fire. Can you give me some ideas to help them?

Motivated in Maine

Dear Motivated,

Motivation comes from inside a person. When motivation is supplied from outside, it is more a form of persuasion or coercion. Many directors believe it's their job to motivate their staff, but it is more productive to harness what it is that brings a staff member to camp in the first place.

During the summer of 1987, I visited almost forty camps throughout the country. From an informal, anonymous survey of more than 2,000 counselors, I was impressed to learn that more that 80 percent listed "wanting to make a difference working with children" as the factor that motivated them most to be at camp. Since then I have noticed that most staff come to camp motivated, but certain conditions wear that motivation away. What follows is a partial list of what I have learned.

Don't leave surprises for staff. Securing staff morale and making the most of motivation begins with the interview or screening process. Directors who don't convey the true conditions of camp life *before* staff sign a contract are setting themselves up for failure. Nothing kills a counselor's enthusiasm faster than unexpected surprises about curfews, time off, job responsibilities, and camp rules.

Counselors, like campers, learn when they listen, but they listen best when they feel heard. Directors who take time to listen to their staff members often have happier staffs whose level of motivation remains high. Remember, *listening* to the experiences of staff is different from *conceding* to all the demands they present. Also, listening to staff is one way to avoid getting into control battles with them, which may be the number one enemy of camp staff motivation.

Staff members who are given real responsibility, with guidance and support, tend to feel trusted and more motivated. Likewise, acknowledging the expertise of staff goes a long way toward building morale and self-confidence and may even prompt many of them to take more initiative at camp. Counselors arrive with a variety of talents and skills. A wise director is flexible enough to fashion parts of the program and special activities for the summer in such a way that staff members get to show off.

Support your staff's efforts to enter the world of campers. While this sounds like a simple matter, it is fraught with potential complications. For example, some staff members may feel self-conscious about dropping their inhibitions to become interested again in things they feel they have outgrown. This is often a problem for young male counselors who work with very young children; they worry about how they might look to other staff (or, more important, how they compare to their own internal image of what a man is). Such counselors need help expanding their image of what is acceptable, with reassurances about how they're mastering the demands of the job.

The flip side to overinhibited staff includes those who let go too much and end up being the camp's biggest kids. The challenge for staff is to be child*like*, not child*ish*. Staff members who sacrifice self-control or good judgment to be popular with campers don't add to the development of impulse control, good judgment, or self-restraint in those children.

There must be a balance here, since one of the assets of a rich camp community is the presence of "character," which is provided by staff members whose role is to keep the morale high at camp. The test is whether staff members can make campers feel invited to share in the fun in a safe way where contributions, ideas, and imagination are valued.

Specific, clear, immediate feedback consistently builds morale. One of the foremost complaints of staff at the more than 250 camps I've visited in the last ten years is the feeling that their efforts go unnoticed by the people they consider to be their bosses. In my survey, more than 90 percent of the counselors said they wanted to impress or please their directors with their job performance.

On the other hand, most directors complain that they don't have time to go around camp complimenting staff. If your number one resource is staff, doesn't it make sense to give high priority to those things that keep morale and enthusiasm high? If you are spending so much time in the office or on other tasks that keep you away from the camper-counselor action, perhaps you are more a camp manager than a camp director.

The single greatest boost a staff member can receive is specific, sincere, immediate recognition of his or her efforts. It is inexpensive, communicates value, and is powerful. General, nonspecific praise, such as, "You guys are doing a great job this season," doesn't have the same impact. Although such comments don't hurt, counselors need specific, individualized feedback.

Camps that have a great disparity between how campers are valued and how counselors are valued tend to have low staff morale. The creation of a happy, safe community means treating *every* member of that community with integrity, interest, fair play, and concern for self-esteem.

Opportunities for Success

1. Director sees potential in young person to be on staff who doesn't always measure up.
2. Make sure she wants the opportunity as much as you want it for her.
3. She has to make the commitment to joining the staff.

Dear Bob,

We have taken a seventeen-year-old young lady from a local family under our wing, so to speak, and have given her a job in our kitchen, as well as opportunities to do activities with some of the younger campers in our all-girls overnight camp. Even though she comes from a tough family situation and never went to camp herself as a child, we see a lot of potential in her. She can be great with the children and has spells of genuine enthusiasm.

The problem is that she sometimes doesn't do her work thoroughly, is late, argues with the cook, and reportedly talks to the children about subjects we consider inappropriate.

Bob, we know how positive camp can be for young adults as well as children, so we hate to give up on her. What do you think might help us help her?

Hopeful

Dear Hopeful,

While I agree that camp can be a powerful setting for staff as well as campers, you may need to go back to basics with your young friend. It sounds like you have given her a great opportunity, accompanied, I am sure, by plenty of support and guidelines. My question is, does she want it? Unless she can say that she truly wants the opportunity you want to give her, you may find yourself wanting something more than she does. I suggest you sit down and ask her if she wants to be at camp. Make it clear that, if she does, you are willing to support her and work with her to help her get what *she* wants.

If, however, she cannot make the commitment, then you have nothing to work with. Tell her that, if she doesn't want to be at camp, that it is okay and that you will help her leave in an appropriate way.

Camp directors are very good at seeing potential in people—especially young people—that others miss. The difficulty comes in turning over the responsibility for success for developing that potential to, in your case, your kitchen helper. It is true that we can become so enamored with other people's potential that we never let them make a commitment because we never ask them to. Without *their* commitment to something they want, we have no partnership with them in the great work that camp can help people do.

Once your friend has decided she does want to be at camp, your job will be much easier, and her vision of what she must work on to be able to stay will be much clearer.

Keeping Returning Staff Involved

1. Involve older staff in planning and leading orientation.
2. Use their expertise.
3. Pay them.
4. Don't drag them through precamp.

Dear Bob,

As a day camp, we often find it difficult to keep our older, experienced staff (who are often schoolteachers) interested during staff orientation. It wouldn't be such a problem if their sometimes negative attitudes weren't so contagious. Any ideas?

Day Camp in the Northeast

Dear Day Camp,

Assemble your management team early in the fall and compile a list of your tried-and-true returning staff members. Then set some dates, to begin in February, for planning your orientation and include some of your experienced regulars. Acknowledging expertise is a powerful way to validate people and get them involved. Back up your expression of confidence by paying them for their time. A nominal fee can go a long way toward putting backbone into your strategy (and can pay off tremendously later).

Have your old-timers work themselves into the orientation schedule by having them lead or colead particular small group sessions (on pool safety, morning lineup, lunch procedures, or comforting a homesick child, for example). If you let them show off, you'll get some spark.

Also, don't drag your old-timers through your entire precamp package. Have a separate session for the new staff only (keep it simple), and then set aside time for old-timers and newcomers to meet and mix. Good luck and happy camping!

Cooldowns for Staff

1. When staff member verbally attacks a camper:
   - balance between protecting camper and intervening in a way that saves face for staffer
   - goal is disengagement and restoring safety
   - move between camper and staff
   - diffuse the explosive situation
2. Assign consequences and get apologies.

Dear Bob,

We operate a camp outside New York City with a population of children who tend to test their limits with our staff. While we carefully screen and train our counselors, occasionally some of them will reach a point where they overreact or lose their cool and scream. How do we respond in a way that protects the camper without destroying the credibility of the staff member?

New York

Dear New York,

You correctly identify the dilemma as a balance between protecting the camper while intervening in a manner that enables the counselor to save face and recover. Since most children are experts at knowing exactly what to do or say to provoke adults, counselors should be prepared for this testing so they won't react to it personally. I use the phrase "Dear Occupant" as a way of making the point with staff during orientation in this way.

Just as we often receive mail marked "occupant," intended for anyone at a given address, children often use us to play out their unresolved feelings. Like the mail we don't want, their antics are addressed to whatever authority figure is handy, mostly as an intuitive way of replaying their behavior until they get a different (hopefully healthier) response. Many counselors, especially less experienced ones, may feel personally attacked by such provocations when, in fact, it is not personal. Children do, however, have extremely sensitive radar and will actually sniff out staff members whose own self-control may be questionable. Helping counselors practice detachment—not the same as disinterest, but rather a way of not taking things personally—can be useful in avoiding such encounters.

So what do you do when a counselor loses control and verbally attacks a child? First of all, remind yourself and your staff that in such situations emotions run high. It is imperative to act quickly, but calmly. The last thing the situation needs is a third party adding to the fervor.

Move toward the counselor and see if you can tactfully place yourself physically between him or her and the child. Remember, when emotions are high, the engagement between the staff member and camper will be intense, so this move is intended to dilute that intensity. Your goal is disengagement. Debriefing, repairs, and reassessment of the staff member will come later.

For now, address only the counselor, not the camper. If you feel you can put a gentle, reassuring hand on the counselor's shoulder and are certain this move will not be perceived as inflammatory, then do so. The goal is to produce a calming, reassuring effect; do nothing that is attacking, judgmental, or threatening, since this may escalate the situation.

The words you use should be designed to signal your concern for the well-being of the staff member. Address the staff member by his or her first name to increase your contact. For example, I often say something like this: "Timmy, how's it going? You seem upset. What's happening?"

The objective is to diffuse this potentially explosive situation without doing to your staff member what he or she may be in the process of doing to the camper. Remember, how you react, especially under pressure, will not be lost on your campers. As we all know, actions speak louder than words.

Once you have diffused the situation, you can go about the business of consequences and apologies as necessary. Make sure the camper knows that, no matter what his behavior may have been, it did not warrant such an attack by the counselor.

113

Counselor Indiscretion

1. Misplaced loyalty confuses campers.
2. Give kids permission to be curious about their interest in sex.
3. Set limits. Curiosity does not mean acting on impulses.

Counselors can be a camp's greatest resource as well as its biggest liability, as is indicated by the following episode from a camp in the Midwest.

Tom (not his real name) is an eighteen-year-old junior counselor who told a sexually explicit and graphic story to a group of ten-year-old boys. Like most children who witness something they are not sure they can manage emotionally, these boys spilled the beans and word of the incident eventually got back to the director.

After due process, the director fired Tom. The question then was what to say to the campers about the story and Tom's departure.

Before considering the main points, we need to consider ten-year-old boys. At this age, most boys are extremely curious about sexual matters, but are embarrassed about admitting it to adults. Furthermore, they easily become overstimulated, which is usually detectable by their silly behavior.

The second thing to know about ten-year-old boys is their sense of loyalty. Because Tom was probably regarded by some of the boys as being cool, many of them will feel responsible for his being fired. Their line of thinking is usually something like this: "If only I could keep a secret, Tom wouldn't have gotten fired." In other words, many kids this age think that it is some basic defect in them that causes them to be disloyal. Unless the issue is addressed, many boys will needlessly suffer in silence. When outside the company of adults, these boys will accuse each other of being defective by insinuating that one can't keep a secret, another is a baby for being put off by the story, and so on.

Knowing what we do about ten-year-old boys, then, our words need to address two issues. The first is to absolve them of the guilt they feel over their imagined responsibility for the firing of the counselor. The second is to help them understand their feelings about the story itself—both their interest in it and their other reactions.

Here's a simple format you can follow when you talk to them.

1. Tell them what Tom did was wrong. While some of the story was probably exciting, and that is natural and okay, it is unfair for adults to say things to kids that get them too excited. Adults are supposed to know when to stop. In fact, they are supposed to help kids learn to do the same thing.

unit three

managing staff

2. Make sure they understand that Tom did not get fired because of them; he got fired because he said things that would make any ten-year-old have feelings that are too strong for them.
3. Let them know that it is okay for them to have mixed feelings about Tom. Children often need help with the notion of mixed feelings. To them it seems impossible to have two or more distinct and sometimes conflicting feelings about one person at the same time. Furthermore, tell them it is okay for some campers to feel one way about Tom and what he said while others feel a totally different way. Feelings are not right or wrong, and everyone is entitled to them. They will need help seeing that it is possible for each one of them to have his own reaction to what Tom did and still be friends with campers whose feelings are different. It is okay to like Tom, to miss him, to be angry at him, or to be glad he is gone. They can even like him and still be glad he is gone. It is also okay not to care one way or the other.

It is also important to address the more secretive feelings they have about Tom's story and their reaction to it. Start out by giving the boys permission to have certain feelings. Most ten-year-olds don't want to linger on the subject of sex any longer than they have to, unless there are no adults around. Here is a sampling of what you might say.

1. Parts of Tom's story may have been exciting or made you curious. Just because you are curious about something, however, doesn't mean someone should take advantage of your curiosity. It's unfair for an adult to say things to children that seem exciting or interesting, but later make you feel uneasy or ashamed.
2. I know most boys don't like to talk about things like Tom's story with adults, so I won't ask you about it, because it is okay for your feelings to be private. Sometimes you hear things, though, that are wrong or that you might not understand, so if anyone wants to talk to me in private, you can let me know and no one else will have to know you are talking to me.

Though most directors prefer to have a fired staff member off the grounds as soon as possible, in a case like this, your repair work with children is actually enhanced if you can manage to have Tom address the group to say the following: what I did was wrong; I need to leave; my leaving is not your fault, it's mine; I'm sorry for what I did because you guys deserve better; the good things we did together are still important and I will take those memories with me.

One compromise is to have the departing counselor write a letter to the campers, which you can then read to them when you tell them he is gone.

One last note has to do with speaking to the rest of the staff about Tom's departure. You might discover you need to cover the same points with them about responsibility and knowing when to stop. After all, we all know that counselors can be your biggest kids.

Defining Appropriate Staff Behavior—Firing Staff

1. Inappropriate behavior that causes a staff member to be fired should be discussed with parents of affected campers.
2. Discuss situation with staff promptly.

Dear Bob,

I have worked as a counselor at a boys' camp for the past two years. During that time I have been uneasy with how the director handles the departure of fired counselors.

His approach is to keep any unpleasant event quiet. I, on the other hand, have always felt a need for some information in order to address campers' concerns. Staff need not be given every detail. But there have been situations where a counselor has literally vanished overnight.

What is your view on how a counselor's departure for inappropriate behavior should be addressed?

Difference of Opinion

Dear Opinion,

It is clear that directors and staff could benefit from an open exchange about the departure of a colleague who has behaved inappropriately. The staff-director partnership can be strengthened, camp values can be reinforced, expectations of appropriate behavior can be clarified, and staff can be prepared to answer questions.

Despite these benefits, I have found damage control to be the single greatest concern of many directors. Directors are afraid that news of a counselor's inappropriate behavior might be detrimental to the trust parents have in the camp or the director. While this is a reasonable fear, in many instances parents are angrier when inappropriate behavior directed toward their child has been covered up. Furthermore, many parents who have been contacted are relieved to know that the director has intervened; the director's openness builds parents' trust.

After all, most parents really want to know three things: Is my child safe? Is the offender gone? Is this the whole truth? Issues not dealt with openly may cause rumors to spread.

Directors may also be concerned about their staff's reaction to the firing of a counselor. I find that staff actually admire directors who take a strong stand when it comes to removing individuals whose behavior jeopardizes the community. Directors never need to hide clear, strong, and forthright decisions.

With these things said, here's my advice to your director.

1. Be prompt about talking with staff. This is about trust, continuity in your program, and rumor control.
2. Be selective about what you share. Staff need to know where they stand with you and what to tell (and not tell) campers.
3. Be up front and direct—it will clear the air.
4. Give credit to your staff for pulling together, helping out, and doing what they do well.

Personnel Management—More on Firing Counselors

> 1. Directors need to gain some emotional distance and allow supervised goodbyes when a counselor is fired.
> 2. Accompany fired person or send a trusted staff member along.
> 3. If time doesn't permit personal goodbye, a note works.

Dear Bob,

Over the past seven years, Camp Counselors USA has been placing counselors at hundreds of camps across America. During this time a very small number of the counselors have been fired.

While I fully understand that not all employee-employer relationships work out, many camps have the policy that fired staff members must leave camp immediately. In many cases the staff member has no chance to say goodbye to campers or colleagues, which can be an emotional disaster if the person is thousands of miles from home.

I understand the camp director's need to eliminate a problem without causing disruption to the camp, but isn't there a more humane way of releasing staff?

Bill Harwood
President, CCUSA

119

Dear Bill,

Your letter understandably focuses on the feelings of counselors who are abruptly asked to leave camp. Most any counselor who is invested in camp, no matter how far away from home, would be upset if they had to leave without saying goodbye to friends. I would add that campers may also suffer from the sudden disappearance of a fired counselor.

Directors, however, are concerned about protecting the envelope of safety they have been working to establish at camp and often feel an urgency to remove a staff member they believe might undermine morale or the camp's values.

There are two procedures directors can use that would allow some closure for the people most closely associated with the counselor in question while protecting that envelope of safety.

First, directors can acknowledge the importance of saying goodbye, both for the counselor and for the children who are close to that counselor. This requires directors to take a deep breath and gain some emotional distance from the situation that brought about the firing in the first place. This is an exercise in reason, the rationale of which is that campers, not just counselors, do better when they can say goodbye. However, it is important for the director or some other less involved but *trusted* member of the senior staff to accompany the fired staff member as he or she takes leave of his or her friends. This way the separation can be kept on track and can be monitored.

In cases where it is not possible for a fired staff member to see campers before he or she leaves, it might be helpful for him or her to write a note to campers that can be read by another staff person. The note should be simple and should contain several items, as follows:

1. The reason the staff member left had nothing to do with anything a camper did or said. In other words, care should be taken that no camper feels responsible in any way.
2. In cases where the counselor did something wrong that involved campers, he or she readily admits it.
3. Even though the counselor is sad to have to go, he or she is glad that camp will continue. He or she knows the children will continue to grow and have fun.
4. Campers should be reassured that the counselor will be fine and is going on to other things.

For the sake of honoring the attachments that people form in a closely knit community like camp, care needs to be taken to strike a balance between the need to protect that community and the need to honor the relationships within it.

120

Defining Appropriate Staff Behavior—Off-Season Contact

> 1. Counselors who see campers off-season to get emotional needs met can lead to problems:
>   - hurt feelings
>   - inadequate supervision
>   - campers with overstimulating attachments (setup for abuse)
> 2. Set policy concerning off-season contact between staff and campers.

Dear Bob,

Last fall we got a call from a parent wanting to know if we were aware that one of our counselors had been taking campers on outings during the off-season (their son had been invited to go along). We, indeed, had not known.

While we have never had a specific policy about this, it does make us uneasy. We don't want to be alarmist, but, with all the concern about child abuse, we feel the need to be cautious. What is your advice?

Wary in Washington

Dear Wary,

While most counselors who pursue friendships with campers during the off-season probably have the best of intentions, it is reasonable for you to be concerned. Most young adults have things they'd rather do with their time than outings with one or more youngsters.

It is important to keep in mind that counselors who are interested in having contact with campers after camp are not necessarily child molesters. Many appropriate friendships between counselors and individual campers continue in some form after camp. However, there are counselors who use children to get more of their own emotional needs met than is healthy. When this is the case, different problems can arise. These problems can include children suffering hurt feelings when not included, not receiving adequate supervision, or developing an overstimulating attachment with the counselor, which can be a setup for potential abuse. Furthermore, some off-duty counselors may get into relationships with children who are more needy or demanding than they can handle. Without the checks and balances that a camp's staff, structure, and supervision provide, they may end up doing something they did not consciously set out to do.

Parents and counselors both need to be made aware of these risks. Make a clear policy statement to staff that you discourage ongoing relationships with campers outside of or after camp. Make it clear to staff that this policy is stated to parents as well. (I do make a distinction between responding to letters campers may write, which is great, and counselors initiating and soliciting a relationship through letters, calls, and visits, which is not encouraged.) When speaking with staff, clarify that your concerns are as much for the staff's safety and well-being as for the campers or the reputation of the camp.

The parents' statement should go out in the early fall and should be written in general terms. You may also want to consult with your lawyer about clarifying the limits of the camp's liability. Always make clear to parents that counselors who pursue such relationships do not represent you or your camp. Encourage parents to call if they have any questions.

If parents decide to allow an outing with a counselor after you have made your concerns clear, that is, of course, their right. However, you might advise that outings be done in groups and always with another adult present. There are clearly limits to your authority in this situation, so it is the power of persuasion that makes the difference.

Some camps offer off-season trips and outings of their own. This provides an alternative to unsupervised, unauthorized gatherings between staff and campers while reinforcing customer loyalty. Camps that have such outings report a decline in the number of incidents where staff independently seek out campers as well as an increase over time in their return rate. It also provides another forum for a camp to bring to life its values and philosophies.

Defining Appropriate Staff Behavior—A Technique for Giving Feedback to Counselors

1. Confronting counselors who bring contraband items for campers.
2. Moving the motivation to do the right thing from external to internal source.

Dear Bob,

We have had trouble with a certain kind of counselor behavior and we would like to hear your ideas. Very often we have a counselor who is very popular with his campers, partly because he insists on bringing candy, food, and other contraband into camp for them. After confronting him about the rules in our camp and getting repeated assurances from him that he will stop, the flow of outlawed items begins anew. What else can we do except fire him, even though that seems too drastic a measure, especially if he is a good counselor in other respects?

Miffed in Michigan

Dear Miffed,

Call the counselor in question into the office and simply ask him when is he going to trust himself. When he asks you what you are talking about, tell him you have been wondering why it is that he thinks his campers like him *only* for the things he brings them. Tell him that, even though you can see some great characteristics in him that most children would admire and be drawn to, he obviously must not feel that way because he seems to be using food and candy to get his campers to like him.

He may protest and disagree but, each time he goes to bring his campers candy or other things, he will think about what you said. When that happens, the argument will be between him and himself, not between you and him. In other words, you will have succeeded in getting under his skin, so to speak, and moving the locus of control from outside of him to inside of him. Changes are always more effective and lasting when they are motivated from within.

Skills for Staff Supervisors

1. Supervisors must all agree on:
   - camper discipline
   - child management techniques
   - expectations
   - policies on drugs, booze, curfew
   - grounds and procedures for firing
   - methods for coaching, supporting, and rewarding staff
2. Role play and discussions among supervisors.
3. Preview new things for supervisors first—it increases their stake in it.
4. Supervisory skills needed:
   - observation
   - confrontation
   - checklisting
   - repair work

With summer fast approaching many directors have been preoccupied with making last-minute staff appointments and preparing for orientation and the arrival of this year's crop of campers. One often overlooked but central area of concern has to do with preparing and training staff supervisors. Because most supervisors don't start new with every camp season, they tend to accumulate knowledge, experience, and expertise that can give your camp program greater depth and stability. These folks serve as a kind of "starter dough" for younger or less experienced staff. Supervisors are the people at camp who reinforce camp policy, philosophy, and culture as it plays out during the season.

Ideally, supervisors should be a part of a staff development program—that is, an ongoing, year-round education and training effort. Whether they have come up through the ranks or have been brought in from another organization, supervisors must truly be in agreement about the range of acceptable behavior in the following important areas at camp.

- Camper discipline and child management techniques
- Expectations for program staff, bunk counselors, and/or group leaders
- Policies on drugs, alcohol, curfew (at residential camps), and so on
- Grounds and procedures for dismissal (e.g., who fires and how does it happen?)
- Methods for coaching, supporting, and rewarding staff

Supervisors need to discuss and role-play particular responses to specific situations at camp, since it is out of these kinds of exercises that they become clear about what is and is not acceptable at camp. Even staff who have been with a camp for several years who think they are clear about camp policy can discover they have wildly divergent views or understandings when they go to put that policy into practice. Slogans and clever sayings can be confusing for much the same reason—when people act, they discover that what was an assumed agreement can turn out to be two very different visions of the same phrase.

Likewise, if you plan to introduce new techniques or procedures or have a substantially new orientation program, it is smart to have your supervisors or key staff experience it first. Besides creating a greater sense of solidarity, exposing your supervisors to new methods or material allows them to digest the information, buy into the ideas, and become more comfortable with any new language and nuances before they have to use them with staff. Having such prior exposure allows supervisors to appear and act more certain and competent. Furthermore, giving key staff/leadership team members a preview of what has been planned for the summer empowers them to take greater ownership in the program, which increases their stake in its success.

Once the supervisory duties begin, key staff will need skills in four significant areas in order to be successful as supervisors: observation, confrontation, use of a checklist, and repair work. Let us look at each of them more closely.

Observation skills are essential for anyone who wants to be effective with people. Indeed, someone who has super vision—one who can see, take in, size up, monitor, and so on—is someone who is a good observer. Being a good observer means many things, including

1. Watching carefully (being present and undistracted)
2. Not drawing premature conclusions
3. Checking out assumptions and appearances
4. Observing one's own biases, likes, and dislikes

One helpful aid for supervisors might be to brainstorm and prepare a kind of guide or grid to use while observing staff. It could include such categories as eye contact, appropriate touch, one-on-one communication, speaking up with camper groups, pitching in, working as a team with cocounselors, and so on. Having a guide helps keep observations more neutral. Such a guide might evolve over time as people use it and identify more distinct or specific categories of counselor behavior.

The second central skill area for supervisors is **confrontation**. Volumes could be written about confrontation skills, and it takes years of practice for most people to do it well. However, a few tips and pointers can serve as a primer for inexperienced or younger supervisors.

To most people, the word "confrontation" has negative connotations, and people become apprehensive when they consider confronting others. Hurt feelings, fears about escalating arguments, and lack of know-how all contribute to this apprehension. Confrontation in its most useful form, however, is not an attack or character assassination, but rather an invitation to look at something together in a spirit of mutual respect. Obviously, when that something is a counselor's own performance, pride and defensiveness can get in the way. Thus, supervisors need to become versed in how to handle the prideful feelings of their staff. This is a necessary consideration because, after all, pride is an innate and valuable part of all human beings. Counselors who have very little pride perform in thoughtless and careless ways. Obviously, it is better when staff are proud of their work. It also means, however, that they may react defensively when criticized or approached about their performance.

Some supervisors, in approaching staff with a sensitive issue, think first of a positive comment they can make before pointing out a shortcoming. While this can be effective, remember that female staff typically remember only negative feedback, while males typically remember only positive feedback.

Another technique is "checking it out." This can be a simple, but effective opening phrase—"Can I check something out with you?" Another useful phrase is, "I was wondering. . . ." For example, "I was wondering if you know that pillow fights weren't something we did here at camp." The language is inclusive and gives the counselor the benefit of the doubt.

Yet another technique is giving benefit of the doubt. "Of course, I know you didn't mean to get carried away, but we need to work harder to keep the noise level down during lunch." Again, the language is inclusive and the approach is not an attack.

When giving feedback to staff, most supervisors use nonspecific language, thus communicating an often unclear message. To avoid this, I suggest the use of a **checklist**. A checklist is a specific way to give more precise feedback. For example, if I were to say to a counselor, "You need to have better contact with the children," what do I really mean? Using a checklist, I can itemize specific behaviors, such as

1. Stand in the middle of your group.
2. Make more eye contact.
3. Speak up sooner.
4. Gather the group together before changing activities.

Checklists should be

- behavior specific
- stated in positive terms
- limited to three or four items, tops
- written down
- followed up

If a counselor is given a checklist of improvements, the supervisor needs to check back a day later to acknowledge progress, give feedback, measure performance, and further refine the process.

In all human endeavors where people work in teams there will be occasional misunderstandings and slipups. That is why all good supervisors should know how to do **repair work.** Repairing a rift or hurt feelings involves several steps.

- Listening patiently (and not taking things too personally)
- Validating feelings ("I can understand why you were hurt." "I'm sorry you felt that way.")
- Giving credit ("I'm glad you are willing to talk about it/come to tell me.")
- Acknowledging the parts that are true ("You are right in that I shouldn't have confronted you in front of everyone—your behavior was out of line, but I could have told you in a better way.")
- Taking ownership ("It was not okay for me to single you out that way.")

All of these skill areas take practice and get better with age. However, if directors are truly intent on giving kids a world of good, they will make sure their supervisors have the skills to make good on the delivery.

127

unit four
parents

Nurse Practitioner, Chauffeur, Bottle Washer, Indian Chief

To understand parents and the encounters we have with them in camping, we have to look at families as a whole and at the pressures and changes they have experienced in the last several years. High divorce rates, domestic violence, one-parent households, or both parents working are common characteristics of families in the United States today.

While the divorce rate for first marriages has stabilized between 10 and 35 percent, the incidence of divorce is unequally distributed across socioeconomic lines. The wealthier families are, the higher the divorce rate. Poorer families simply cannot afford the legal fees and division of resources that for them are scarce to begin with. This means that camps that deal with families that have higher incomes will have higher divorce rates and the problems that come with them—youngsters with torn loyalties, custodial parents forbidding noncustodial parental contact, arguments about who is financially responsible, worries (real or imagined) of kidnaping by estranged parents, and so on. Camps that have a poorer clientele have a lower divorce rate, but may have children who show signs of stress disorders and trauma from domestic violence, alcoholism, or abandonment.

Just as alarming is the fact that parents spend up to 40 percent less time with their children today than in the late 1970s. Up to 72 percent of families don't know the neighbors in their own communities, and, if mom and dad still are together, they end up spending about twenty minutes a day together as a couple. Children, meanwhile, spend only about fifteen minutes a day with their parents, much of it with parents desperately trying to get them to stop hitting their siblings, pick up their clothes, get ready for school, or turn off the TV. Mary Pipher, in her book *The Shelter of Each Other* (G. P. Putnam's Sons, 1996), describes parents and families as being "thirsty in the rain." While parents may have more money, TVS, VCRs, and phones, they have less time, less security, and less of a sense of well-being for their children. For all of the affluence in the United States (corporate profits are at a thirty-year high and the GNP is a robust $6 trillion plus[1]), parents are less certain about the future, health, and safety of their children than ever before.

Indeed, parents of the 1990s struggle with deciding what is the right thing to do with their children. For example, when parents forbid chil-

130

---

1. "Does America Still Work," *Harper's Magazine,* May 1996, pp. 40–41.

dren to watch TV shows with violent themes, not only do their children rebel with an outraged sense of deprivation, but parents realize their children will see and hear these shows or experience their effects anyway. All the kids from the homes where Power Rangers is a "blocked" show go to the kids' homes where it is standard fare. In school, all the tricks and kicks of the show are replayed as a regular part of the children's culture. Unless *all* parents block the show, most kids will still end up emulating the violence.

All of this has produced children who, socialized by the 400 or so ads they see or hear each week,[2] are much more rude, impulsive, self-centered, and sexually precocious than their counterparts of even five years ago. As a result, parents have grave concerns about safety and keeping their children out of trouble. The first and foremost concern parents have about sending their children to camp is, will he or she be safe? Camps that fail to recognize this concern lose customers. Second, given the unstable and dangerous climate in which parents perceive their children growing up, coupled with the lack of time they have to be with their children, parents today demand a different kind of contact with their children than camps have traditionally been comfortable with (having weekly phone calls; making phone calls on birthdays and special occasions; taking children out of camp on visiting days or keeping children home from day camp certain days of the week). I certainly am not arguing that camps should totally give themselves over to all parental demands. However, today's directors need to be aware of the concerns behind these demands and be creative about how to provide parents with solutions that work for them, their child, and the camp. Parents are also loathe to share certain personal information about their children with camp professionals (bed-wetting, hyperactivity, learning disabilities, problems with being overly aggressive) for fear that their children won't be accepted at camp.[3]

What these trends amount to for camping professionals is the need to include parents as partners in this adventure called "camp." Rather than shunt parents aside with the belief that camp magic happens best with them out of the picture, we need to consult, hear, and appreciate parents. While it is true that parents need to let their children go and that children can master a wonderful sense of autonomy and self-reliance when this happens, struggling with or judging parents will not promote the process in a positive way. This is in part because parents are, in some ways, looking for a different product—one that speaks to their concern for their children to grow up and develop in a safe environment where parents and their input are valued almost as part of a

2. Hillary Clinton, *It Takes a Village* (New York: Simon & Schuster, 1996).

3. See "Getting Better Information" (January 1989) and "Requesting Personal Information from Parents" (January–February 1994) elsewhere in this book.

team. This is especially true for working parents who struggle with their guilt about not being as involved in their children's lives as they might like.[4]

Camping professionals who have learned to speak to parents' desire for a growth experience for their children and who can allay the guilt, insecurity, or uncertainty common among American parents are the ones whose reenrollments and communitywide reputations are thriving. Disarming parental anger, reframing negative comments or actions to reveal a hidden positive concern ("Look, the reason you keep calling me is not because you are a pest; it's because you want what's best for your children."), and encouraging parental feedback are all tools of the savvy director. Expressing gratitude even for hostile phone calls and reiterating the need for partnership ("I'm glad you called—it's the parents we don't hear from that we are concerned about. Let's work on this together.") go hand in hand with acknowledging parents' expertise ("Look, *you* know Susie best. What do you think could work within the context of our program here at camp?") and validating parents' feelings ("Of course you're upset—the situation you describe can't be easy."). These are the tools that make a difference with parents—ones that fit the spirit and positive regard for children and parents embodied in the material that appears in this unit.

132

4. Robert Reich, U.S. Secretary of Labor, points out that two parents work, in part, to keep their heads above water financially (*Harper's*, op cit).

unit four

parents

Encouraging Parents to Disclose Sensitive Information

1. Parents are reluctant to disclose sensitive information about their children because they fear:
   - you won't accept him or her to camp
   - you won't treat him or her like a normal kid
   - parents are sworn to secrecy
   - information won't be kept confidential
2. On the camp's personal information form show concern for these normal parental fears and state that you only have their child's interests in mind.
3. Tell who will be privy to information.
4. Address those parent concerns with empathy and respect in a precamp cover letter.

Dear Bob,

I have been a camp director for just under eight years. In that short amount of time it seems that children have been coming to camp with more and more baggage. One difficulty I have is getting accurate, helpful information from parents. I can't tell you how often a child comes to camp without any prior notice from his or her parents that there is a medication or bed-wetting issue. This is information that, had I known about it, could have made their child's adjustment to camp much easier.

Do you have any ideas about how to get parents to tell us what we need to know to help us do a better job with the children put into our care?

Muddled in Minnesota

Dear Muddled,

To get better results from parents who withhold information about their children, you must first begin to think like a parent thinks. Parents do not disclose what seems to us to be crucial information about their children for what seems to them to be good reasons. These reasons need to be approached with respect if you are to make changes. They can be boiled down to the following four concerns:

1. You won't accept our child at your camp if we tell you the truth.
2. You will treat our child with prejudice instead of the way you would treat a normal child.

3. Our child has sworn us to secrecy because he or she is so embarrassed.
4. We cannot trust that the information we share will be kept confidential.

If not openly addressed with parents, these fears continue to operate in a hidden way to inhibit parents from divulging sensitive information about their children. In other words, unless you openly *hear* and *acknowledge* the fears and concerns parents have, they simply will not be able to *hear you* when you state that you need to know this information to be able to help their children adjust. Once the fears are addressed, then and only then will parents be able to be more forthcoming with personal information about their children.

I suggest that you change your form requesting personal information to include a short paragraph where you mention that "...many parents are hesitant to share personal information about their child for fear that their child may be denied enrollment or that such information will prejudice us against their child." Stating this directly will get the subject out in the open.

Continue by noting that "...other parents are understandably concerned about just who will be privy to this information, while still others wonder whether certain problems might not just disappear if not a lot of attention is drawn to them."

Reassure parents that you are not asking for information to be intrusive or to screen campers out. Explain that what you are doing is looking for ways to help with what every parent wants for his or her child—as successful an adjustment to camp as possible. This is important because some parents think that you are just being nosy by asking for personal information. I often tell parents that they are right—it *is* none of my business, and that the only reason I need to know is so I can better help them and their child. I find that making people right opens doors.

You must then be clear about just whom you will share this information with. It is reasonable for parents to want to be somewhat protective of their child's privacy, and it is also often not necessary for anyone in camp other than the director, unit director, nurse, and cabin/bunk/group counselor to know that Johnny has a bed-wetting problem, that Katie has a history of abuse, or that Tom and Sally are from a divorced family. It is, of course, imperative that the staff members with whom you share sensitive information be impressed with the trust being given them and the need for them to guard and respect this trust. I have always found that counselors truly rise to the occasion when we trust them in serious and important ways.

I also strongly suggest that the child be told who in camp knows about his or her private difficulty so that there is no need to be secretive if some need arises once at camp. This also gives the child some sense of control, which can only be helpful in terms of making a smoother adjustment to camp.

In cases where parents have promised their children that they would not tell anyone at camp, more work will need to be done. Parents need help seeing that children do not always know what is in their best interest, and, while you can understand a child's worry and sense of privacy, making such a promise is to be held hostage by a child's fears. This inadvertently confirms for a child that the problem is, indeed, unspeakably shameful. It also suggests that people at camp cannot be trusted to be helpful or careful about the child's well-being. This is not a good message to send a child about the folks with whom he or she is about to spend part of the summer.

Parents will then need help from you to find the words to use with their children when revealing that they cannot keep this promise. It might go something like, "The reason I/we promised in the first place was because we love you and we want your privacy to be protected. *And it will be protected.* The only people in camp who know are [name the exact people]. They have promised us it will never be brought up unless there is a problem, and then only to help you and never to hurt you. It will never be talked about in such a way that other people will find out."

Children today do come to camp with greater troubles. I find increasing numbers of boys on Ritalin, more girls on antidepressants, and many children with histories of trauma and divorce. The fact that camp can be a refuge and even a fresh start for many children should not be confused with the myth that "if we don't talk about it, it will go away." If we *do* talk about it when we need to, it will go away—or at least, in terms of camp, it will not get in the way. And as you know, but many parents do not, a positive camp experience can help a child recover from many run-ins with life. However, the experience must get off on the right foot if it is to be successful, and that means having enough accurate information to get the job done.

I have found that, when parents are approached directly, but with empathy and respect, they respond. After all, most parents want what is best for their children. Creating a partnership with parents rather than an adversarial relationship is crucial to that end.

135

Parents Expect Honesty

1. Abusive behavior such as a male counselor attempting to fondle a female camper should be dealt with forthrightly.
2. Call all parents in the affected group; parents would rather hear from directors than from kids or grapevine.

Dear Bob,

We want to share a situation with you that came up at our residential camp last summer. We think it will interest other camp directors.

After an overnight trip, we learned that a male counselor who slept near a female camper put his hand in her sleeping bag and attempted to fondle her.

After confirming the alleged wrongdoing, we did several things, most of which centered around reassuring the child, dealing with the counselor, and, of course, calling the girl's parents.

In previous articles you have suggested that directors also call the parents of the campers in this girl's cabin, since it was a good bet she had spoken to some of her friends about the incident. We did not look forward to making these phone calls.

Bob, their response was tremendous. Every parent we spoke with was grateful that we had been so direct with them. Some parents told us they expected nothing less from us and wished our policy of openness and direct action could be adopted by their children's schools.

We felt we ended up with a greater friendship and bond with the parents than we had before the incident. Please tell directors that it pays to be proactive with parents. Any camp director's fears that parents might retaliate by removing their children, not reenrolling them, or being aggressive toward camp directors are probably unfounded.

Amy Stein
Echo Lake Camp, New York

Dear Amy,

Your experience matches those that have been shared with me by a myriad of camp directors. Parents do not like bad news any more than the rest of us, but they like it even less coming from their children or through the grapevine when they feel it should have come from you.

It is understandable that directors might feel uneasy or hesitant to share certain events with parents. In some cases, I agree that parents do not need to hear about every problem that comes up at camp. However, if there has been a situation that directly involves the safety or well-being of their child or the cabinmate of their child, it is imperative that they be contacted by you *by telephone* as soon as possible.

Why contact the other parents? Can you imagine if your son or daughter lived with a child who had a traumatic episode at camp? How would you feel if you didn't hear about it from the director? Parents feel ambushed by such a revelation coming from their children (not from the director) three or four months after the fact. In addition to feeling that you're trying to hide something, parents can be left feeling unprepared to help their own children with reactions they may have to what they may have witnessed or heard about.

My rule is this: if it isn't a problem, don't make it one; but if it is a problem, don't duck it. Parents of children who share living space with a child who suffers some kind of trauma at camp will be grateful that you took the time to fill them in on things. What parents want to know is very simple: Is my child safe? Has the situation been corrected? What are the chances of this happening again?

Parents who sue or retaliate against directors are those who feel you have something to hide. Saul Rowen, a camp director from California, said, "Bob, you can't emphasize enough how important it is to be up front with parents. We had a child abuse situation come to light after camp a few summers ago, and I had to contact several parents whose children had been involved. It was tough, but they were grateful that I didn't try to avoid them or cover anything up. In fact, they were extremely supportive, and they empathized with my problems of having to deal with many families."

Directors tell me parents say things such as, "It's refreshing to have you be so honest with us." One parent even said, "This happened to me when I was sixteen; I know these things can happen."

Still, many directors are concerned about saving face, not only with parents, but with other camps.

"Too often, camp directors feel this should be a closed topic," said Rowen. "They feel it portrays something negative about them or their camp operation when a situation like this occurs. I say, 'You know what? It happens to us, too! Since we deal with children and have adult supervisors, we will continue to be exposed to this problem.'"

Does this mean that you contact the parents of *every* camper after a traumatic event at camp? My strong suggestion is **no**. If it isn't a problem, don't make it one. Occasionally, the parent of a child not directly involved may bring it up, in which case you deal with it at that time. To send word out to everyone arouses the fears or worries of parents who would not otherwise need to be concerned.

In this world of cover-ups and authorities that lack accountability, parents appreciate straight talk from directors. Most parents send their children to your camp for just that reason.

A tip from day camp folks: Most parents get calls from camp only when their child is in need or having some kind of difficulty. While director at Noble's Day Camp in the Boston area, Peter Kerns instituted a new practice that had a strong, positive impact on the entire camp community. He instructed his staff to take a specified number of minutes each day to call parents to tell them about some success or new thing their child had done or completed at camp. Parents were amazed and pleased and felt more a part of what their children were doing at camp. Children felt proud and closer to their counselors as a result. In the words of one parent, "How great to hear something positive! We usually get calls only when something's wrong."

The practice can be utilized at sleep-away camp just as effectively, and the phone seems to have more impact than a letter or note (faster, too). If each staff person slowly works his or her way through the group or bunk, every parent will have heard from camp by the end of a session. Camps keep logs of these calls just to make sure they all get done and to keep track of what is being communicated. Counselors also get a boost from these calls. After all, it is much more fun sharing success with parents than making the usual call because something is not working.

Advice for Parents on Teens

How should parents handle teens?
1. Be clear—consistent, emphasize positive consequences, start early
   - state expectations
   - stay out of arguments
   - restate expectations and leave (detach)
2. Pick your battles—don't expect perfection.
3. Respect teens' need for privacy—emotional distance—they are establishing their own mental lives and boundaries.
4. Don't embarrass teens in front of their friends.
5. Have your own life away from the moods of teens.

Dear Bob,

Do you have some rules of the road for camp directors to put in our newsletters to help parents of teenagers be more effective and confident in dealing with their teens? We hear a lot of distress and uncertainty from parents of teens and would like to have some helpful responses.

Ann Woods
Roughing It Day Camp
Orinda, California

Dear Ann,

Many parents are baffled by the sudden changes and mood swings that overtake their children when they become teens—children, who just yesterday seemed so affectionate and available. The rules of the road I offer can be utilized just as effectively by camp counselors as by parents. So here we go.

Rule One: Be clear about what you expect and what consequences there are for various specific behaviors. Time and time again it is confusion, lack of clarity, and lack of consistency that trips up most parents and counselors in their work with teens. A few quick subrules:

1. The more **consistent** you are with teens, the more they can count on where you are coming from and the less they have to test you.

2. Include **positive consequences** and positive expectations, not just negative ones. Reward what is working and what they are doing right, like getting good grades or helping out around the house.
3. **Start early!** Parents who institute firm limits *after* their children become teens face more of an uphill battle than they would have if those limits had been in place when their children were younger.

The technique I have found most effective with teens when it comes to setting limits or stating expectations is as follows:

1. **State your expectation or limit.** For example, a parent might say, "Cheryl, I expect you in at midnight—no later!" A counselor might say, "Guys, I expect to see you at your next activity in five minutes!"
2. **Stay out of arguments.** Most teens at this point will throw out a variety of reactions like "It's not fair! You're ruining my life! You always let Tony [Alice] stay out late [get away with cutting corners]! This stinks!" You get the idea. These are simply verbal traps. Once you start arguing with a teen when stating your expectation, you're dead. (That's a psychological term meaning, "You've been had!") Simply move on to the next point.
3. **Calmly restate your expectation and leave (detach).** If teens can't argue with you, they have only themselves to argue with. My experience is that, except with especially troubled or angry/defiant teens, this method works 90 percent of the time. At camp, when teens do not respond to this technique, it is then time to move to the next level of response, which is a little "fireside chat" with the unit leader or comparable administrator.

Rule Two: Pick your battles. While it is true that parents and counselors need to be able to say "no" to teens just as they do to younger children, they need to change the context and delivery with teens. For example, a teen who gets home within five or ten minutes of a curfew is essentially complying with that curfew. Expect *responsiveness*, not *perfection*. Most teens are trying to establish their autonomy and feel the need to assert their independence from parents (or parental authority). Becoming ever more vigilant or rigid will only increase resentment and may force some teens to act out their need for independence.

Rule Three: Respect a teen's need for privacy and emotional distance. Remember that teens are establishing their own private mental lives. Up to this point these children have been accustomed to sharing many of their thoughts with parents. However, as a result of both their desire to establish their autonomy and the fact that they are typically experiencing a greater degree of sexual thoughts and feelings, they can become moody and secretive and usually stop sharing with their parents or adult authorities. Many parents and counselors take it personally when teens cut them off or stop sharing their private thoughts. However, this is just a healthy emergence of boundaries.

Some counselors err by going the other way—sharing the details of their private romantic lives with teens as a way of winning popularity or friendship. Obviously, a counselor who does this is insecure and risks overstimulating teens by divulging such information. My advice to counselors who are asked by teens to talk about their private romantic lives is simply to say, "I think you will find that, when you care about someone, you won't go around telling people what you do with them in private."

Rule Four: Don't embarrass them in front of their peers. One of the most important principles for working with teens is not to humiliate or embarrass them in front of their peers. Many parents have noticed that their *simply existing* embarrasses their teens, a condition that is generally most acute for girls who are eleven through thirteen and boys twelve through fourteen. Respect goes a long way here. The issue has to do with teens' desire not to appear to their friends to be too dependent on their parents (and therefore still babies). Choose your moment to reprimand or to talk with your teen(s).

One further note along this line: Anyone who works with teens successfully knows that adults always have two separate relationships with teens—the more private, one-on-one relationship and the more public relationship when they are in the presence of their peers. Again, the issue is potential embarrassment caused by drawing too much attention to the attachment a teen has with you. Contrary to their exterior bravado and often surly attitude, teens become very attached to some adults. They simply want those adults to be cool about that attachment (i.e., not to make a big deal out it by drawing attention to that fact).

Rule Five: Have a life of your own. Parents of teens need their own emotional outlets and relief from the storms and moods of their teenage children. I always recommend that parents of teens get to know other parents of teens. They often find out their youngster isn't so bad, after all. This advice is especially true for counselors who work with teens. Having your own identity, friends, and social life is the best defense against the regressive pull teens can exert on people who work closely with them.

What I have found in the twenty years I have worked with teens is that they are looking for authority figures they can look up to—people who have a sense of themselves and who are firm, clear, and unafraid to say "no" when they need to, but who are also warm and respectful in the process.

Kissing Camper

Confronted with precocious sexual behavior by a camper, directors should:
1. Consult the parents first. They need to be involved, especially in day camps.
2. Help parents not to over- or underreact.

Dear Bob,

We had an eight-year-old boy at our day camp last summer who had a habit of kissing female counselors and attempting to touch their breasts. He also seemed to have some precocious knowledge of sexual matters, which was of some concern to us. How would you deal with such a child?

Musing in Massachusetts

Dear Musing,

Whatever your intervention with an eight-year-old at a day camp, it should be preceded by a consultation with the parents. When a child this young demonstrates such behavior, it is a clear sign of involvement in an overstimulating sexual incident. This could include seeing a copy of a pornographic magazine; having witnessed some behavior such as that of an older sibling with a boyfriend or girlfriend or that of parents; or actually having a sexual experience with another child, teenager, or adult. This is, therefore, something parents need to know about.

Parents need to be told for two reasons. The first is because they have rights and responsibilities as parents. The second is that getting the boy to comply with limit setting at camp will be a direct result of messages he receives from his parents about his need to comply. Without an alliance with parents, especially in a day-camp situation where he reenters the parents' world every day, you have nothing to work with.

The trick is to help parents to neither overreact nor underreact. This involves being firm and persistent, remaining as businesslike as possible, and educating them about the meaning of such behavior as I have done here. Remind them that his behavior does not make him a bad boy or a cute one, but rather a boy in need of help.

143

unit five

child abuse and other sensitive issues

Extending the Envelope of Safety

Child abuse has been one of the more daunting and challenging issues for camping professionals in recent years. The concern about child abuse in camping developed as the result of several key factors. In the late 1960s and early 1970s, mental health professionals and child-care specialists began questioning the use of corporal punishment and other child-rearing practices, some of which were considered abusive to children. Concurrent with this fresh look at parenting was an evolving awareness of child sexual abuse among child and family therapists, with increased press coverage that eventually led to greater public awareness of the problem. By 1978 a presidential commission delivered a report on child abuse naming it one of the most significant social problems in America. Several recommendations were made in that report that were aimed at educating the general public, pediatricians, and hospital emergency room personnel as well as children themselves. (One outcome of these recommendations was the "Good Touch/Bad Touch" curriculum designed for elementary school-aged children.)

Camping professionals came into the loop in the second half of the 1980s. In June 1987, the *Camp Director's Guide* was published as a joint effort by ACA and the Center for Missing and Exploited Children, based in Washington, D.C. This landmark publication was preceded by a three-part series of articles in ACA's *Camping Magazine*, beginning in January 1986 on the types of abuse, methods of detecting abuse at camp, staff interviewing techniques, techniques for working with parents and families, and other topics of this nature. By 1987, with high-profile abuse cases continuing to appear in the media, child abuse had become a hot topic among camping professionals at ACA national and regional conferences, where major sessions about abuse began to appear as regular features for several years to come.

Several particular areas of concern about child abuse have emerged in camping experience. For example, it has become clear that day camps are more likely to see children who evidence signs of neglect, physical abuse, or sexual abuse occurring in the child's family, whereas boys' residential camps have had more difficulties with the potential of abuse at camp. Overall, the incidence of child abuse is extremely low at most camps, though questions remain about disclosure by campers of abuse at home or poor judgment on the part of counselors with regard to camper contact and camper discipline. Here is a list of areas of potential difficulty in various camp settings, including potential victims or players.

Day Camps

- Evidence of neglect: requires reporting to appropriate child protection agency.
- Evidence of physical abuse: requires reporting to appropriate child protection agency.
- Evidence of sexual abuse: requires reporting to appropriate child protection agency.
- Disclosure of abuse (usually by a female camper, often to a friend first, then to a counselor): child and her confidants need to be stabilized; appropriate agency notified; possible family involvement.
- Disclosures occur when a child, feeling safe at camp, tells a staff member or fellow camper of a situation in which he or she has been the victim of physical or sexual abuse.
- Potential sexual abuse of younger children, especially vulnerable because of their age, innocence, dependency on adults, lack of awareness, and so on. May result in a report, investigation, work with the family, and so on.
- Typical areas of vulnerability:
  Overnights
  Overnight travel programs
  Changing times for the pool or other activities
  Bathroom duty with younger children (three to five years old)
  Transportation, where a child may end up alone with an adult in a car, bus, or van
- When children are victimized at day camp, it is usually a one-time occurrence where the victim is young, dependent, or immature. Boys are victimized eleven times more often outside of the family (by a nonfamily member whom, 95 percent of the time, the child knows well and trusts). Disclosures at day camp are often made by females since they are far more likely to be abused inside the family (by a cousin, stepbrother, stepfather, mother's boyfriend). With both boys and girls, 95 percent of the time the offender is a heterosexual male.

Boys' Residential Camps

- Far fewer episodes of observation of signs of neglect or physical or sexual abuse than day camp, though camps who have campers from homes where there is domestic violence or alcoholism have a higher incidence rate of such cases.
- Few disclosures, most often about physical abuse.
- Potential sexual abuse of boys nine to eleven by a staff member (who 90 percent of the time is a heterosexual male, usually very well known to the child).

- Areas of vulnerability for sexual abuse:
  - Overnights at camp
  - Overnights at outposts
  - Shower or changing times
  - Travel programs involving an overnight
  - Overly strong camper-counselor relationship (counselor overidentifies with and gets needs met by camper)
  - Hazing activities or initiation rites
- Areas of vulnerability for physical abuse:
  - Cabin cleanup
  - Pillow fights or wrestling matches where staff participate
  - Overly stressed counselor
  - Especially needy, demanding, or immature camper testing the limits of staff members

Girls' Residential Camps

- Disclosure of abuse, especially sexual abuse, is most prevalent child abuse issue, with girls eight to fourteen most commonly the reporters (see disclosure details on pages 164–165).
- Sexual abuse of females is much less common at camp; female victims are most often abused within their families.
- When sexual abuse of girls occurs at camp, it is usually among eleven to fourteen-year-olds, most often perpetrated by male staff, although female staff who overidentify with and get emotional needs met by female campers may also become offenders.
- Areas of vulnerability:
  - Extended trips, overnights outside of camp
  - Male staff spending too much individualized time with female camper

Generally speaking, coed camps have patterns that are a combination of what is seen in single-sex residential camps. In residential camps, child victims tend to be children who are needy or lack warmth, love, or affection at home; are grieving the loss of a parent through divorce, separation, or death; have problems with boundaries and assertiveness (e.g., have trouble saying "no" to an offender); or are especially vulnerable because of a physical or mental handicap or illness.

Children who are or have been abused at camp may signal their distress through their behavior. Often the abuse is not revealed or disclosed until after camp, when the offender continues to establish contact with the victim during the off-season. At that time, children may become fearful or moody, especially after receiving a phone call or letter from an offender. They may also begin to have nightmares and experience difficulty in school—being distracted, irritable, and isolated and performing poorly. Such children may become clingy, may have trouble leaving the house, and may begin to do things like sleep in their clothes.

Children who are being or have been abused at camp may also show signs of stress while camp is still in session. A sudden change in behavior, such as having recurrent homesickness (after having not been homesick), having a fear of being touched or approached by others, isolating themselves, sleeping in their clothes, or having nightmares may be signs of abuse. Such changes actually signal one of three possibilities: experiencing sexual abuse at camp; receiving disturbing news from home; being teased, bullied, or humiliated by campers or staff. Teenage victims may evidence provocative, often sexualized or even self-abusive behavior, while younger victims may appear or act overstimulated, overly aggressive, or hyperactive.

It is true that years ago children did not make up false allegations regarding abuse. However, with so much media coverage and talks with adults about appropriate touch, children today are more aware and sometimes do fabricate accusations. In addition, with children in the United States watching upwards of four hours a day of unsupervised television and being bombarded by as many as 400 radio, television, and print ads a week, children today are being found by adults to be generally more rude, more sexually aware, more easily bored, and more self-centered, along with having shorter attention spans than they had even five years ago.

The upshot of this has been, among other things, that children who occasionally accuse counselors of having inappropriate sexual contact with them do so because they are angry; are not getting their way; have a crush on a staff member who is ignoring their advances; are having a flashback or fear reaction based on a prior noncamp experience of abuse; or feel jealous or somehow slighted. While this is a rare occurrence in camp settings, it does behoove staff members to follow a fairly clear and rigorous set of guidelines regarding their contact with campers, partly as a way to avoid confusion on the part of campers and partly to minimize the chances of being falsely accused of an impropriety. Some of these guidelines follow:

Guidelines for Camper-Counselor Contact (specific guidelines for touching campers)

- On the arm, shoulder, or upper back
- Never against a child's will (unless in the case of clear and present danger to the child)
- Never against a child's verbally or nonverbally expressed discomfort
- In the company of other adults
- Never when it would have the effect of overstimulating a child
- Never in a place on a child's body that is normally covered by a bathing suit, unless for a clear medical necessity, and then *only with supervision by another adult.*

149

Other Guidelines for Staff

- There is no hazing of campers by campers or counselors.
- Campers will not be subjected to initiation rites that are abusive in any manner.
- There will be double coverage of campers by adults during changing times.
- Younger children should be encouraged to change their own clothes as much as possible.
- Counselors will not give back rubs unless another adult is present and the child is fully clothed.
- Tickling or teasing a camper to the point where that camper is out of control is unacceptable.
- Pillow fights or wrestling matches and the like can become overstimulating in short order and need to be limited and carefully supervised.
- Overnights need a minimum of two adult leaders. At least one counselor present must be of the same gender as the campers.
- Counselors sleeping together on overnights is grounds for dismissal.
- Romantic lives of counselors can, under no circumstances, be shared with campers.
- Male staff working with adolescent females need to be aware of the tendency for members of this group to develop hidden or secret romantic fantasies.
- *Whatever is done with campers should be done in broad daylight, with company!*

150

These guidelines were developed from years of experience with abuse-related situations at camp. For example, at a northern Midwest boys' residential camp several years ago, a counselor took his cabin of nine-year-olds to an outpost cabin for an overnight. The trip was a reward for having had the best score for cabin cleanup inspection for the week, and the boys were excited about it. On the hike out, one boy's sleeping bag became wet from a rainstorm and he had no dry bag to sleep in. There was one bed in the cabin which the counselor was going to use. His solution was to have the boy sleep with him, which is what happened. The next morning when the boys returned to camp, the nine-year-old who had slept with the counselor accused him of fondling him. Though it was never proven one way or the other, the allegation created havoc for the camp, the accused offender, and the cabin group. Had there been two counselors on the overnight, the situation could still have occurred, but double coverage on overnights has other advantages for safety. However, if the counselor had made some other provision, the situation would never have arisen.

At a girls' residential camp in the Northeast several years ago, one twelve-year-old camper disclosed a secret to a bunkmate. The secret—

that this girl had been visited during the night while she was sleeping by a "family friend" who "touched me in private places"—was far more news than the cabinmate had bargained for. After several days the friend swore her counselor to secrecy and then passed on the upsetting news. Obviously disturbed and troubled by it, the counselor nevertheless was torn by her oath of loyalty. When she finally went to the director, a week had passed since the original disclosure.

Sorting through the events helped establish protocol for handling such upsetting disclosures by campers to other campers or staff. First, staff are encouraged not to give blanket confidentiality to campers, saying instead something like, "I'll be happy to keep a confidence as long as it isn't about you being hurt or about you hurting yourself or someone else." (This approach is often used in counselor-counselor-level relationships as well.) Second, when a camper discloses a secret from another camper, counselors have recourse, which is to say, "I think your friend told you because part of her wants help and doesn't want to be alone with her news," and "What kind of friend(s)/counselor would I/we be if I/we didn't help her?"

Furthermore, when hearing a disclosure, adults need to respond with sensitivity, clarity, and confidence (even though it is often a very emotionally charged interaction). Since feelings do run high in these encounters, it helps to have some guidelines, as follows (stated in this order):

1. I am glad you told me/us.
2. What is happening/has happened is not your fault.
3. It is not right.
4. You deserve to get help and be safe.
5. There are people who help children with these kinds of problems (because it does happen to other children).

After making a plan, a report usually must be made within twenty-four hours to the local or state child protective agency. Since 1976, all states have passed mandatory reporting laws which are essentially the same from state to state. Most camp operators know they are mandated reporters, and most cultivate a relationship with the regional intake worker or local office before an incident arises. Some camps invite someone from the office to address staff during orientation, as a way both to convey information and develop some kind of working relationship should it ever be needed in the future.

These and other more detailed tools and strategies are reflected in this unit, which addresses other questions of abuse at camp. By knowing these tools and strategies and reading other materials, camping professionals seem to have been able to minimize the problem of child abuse at camp, preserving a sense of trust and emotional safety in the camp setting.

Protecting our Campers: How to Recognize Various Forms of Child Abuse

1. Child abuse takes many forms:
   - incest
   - sexual abuse/child molesting
   - physical abuse (a.k.a. battered child syndrome)
   - neglect and emotional abuse
2. Screening for abusers—criminal and reference checks, questions on applications re prior convictions.
3. Abusers were usually abused themselves
   - make unrealistic demands (perfectionistic), are authoritarian—not team players
   - often have genuine desire to help kids but handle them harshly
   - use children to validate own needs
4. Child molesters are tuned into kids' needs and skilled at putting kids at ease
   - don't have adult relationships
   - cite relaxing or productive time with kids as their idea of time off
   - drifters or loners with gaps in employment history and frequent job changes
5. Directors can screen for abusers in interviews
   - standardize—all staff using same form of interview
   - don't put candidate at ease too soon
   - ask personal questions late in interview
   - use hypothetical situations and see how candidate would handle them; don't give nonverbal signals as they respond
   - red flags
     candidate tries to control flow of interview as a form of avoidance
     no peer support group
     not team players
     too much free time spent with kids

Since the 1980s the issue of child abuse has mushroomed to the point where it has created grave concern for camp directors and has shaken the camping industry itself. While the actual incidence of this phenomenon may, in fact, be no greater recently than in years past, improved methods of detection and mandated reporting have resulted in exposés that have whipped the national conscience to somewhat of a fevered pitch. Stories from across the country about neglect and abuse at day-care centers and other child-centered agencies have resulted in articles in national publications such as one that paraphrased the thinking of a child molester as follows:

> If you want to ride horses, you go to a stable.
> If you want to molest children, you go to schools, camps and day-care centers.[1]

Suddenly, camp directors—themselves puzzled, concerned, and outraged by these events—find themselves in the uncomfortable position of the potentially accused, while their camps are at risk for a possible disaster that even the insurance companies are afraid to cover. After years of safeguarding the growth and well-being of young people through their profession and avocation, camping professionals face a barrage of penetrating and troubling questions from parents, the media, and others demanding guarantees of immunity from this threat. In the camping community itself, a feeling of concern is often accompanied by frustration and a sense of helplessness as directors and other camping professionals struggle with the questions they face.

My belief is that there are practical, sensible answers to these questions. With clear answers and a rational approach to the problems raised by the headlines of recent years, there is a very real way to eliminate hysteria, reduce feelings of frustration and helplessness, and increase the likelihood of continued safe summers at camp.

There is often confusion about just what it is that constitutes child abuse, as well as exactly what kind of abuse is referred to by such a general term. Child abuse actually refers to three different categories or phenomena—incest, sexual abuse or child molesting, and physical abuse. Two related syndromes are neglect and psychological or emotional abuse—these are not always included under the term "child abuse," but it is important to discuss them in this context. Sexual abuse and physical abuse are probably of greatest concern to camping professionals, although signs of neglect or incest are important, especially to day camp personnel. However, one of the difficulties about child abuse is that it raises such strong feelings in most people that it makes it difficult to discuss it in a rational, coherent, and sensible way. Being clear about these terms is an important first step to minimizing hysteria. When screening for child abuse, it is important to be specific about terms, since the characteristics of a child molester are different from those of a physical abuser.

Incest

Incest refers specifically to sexual acts among family members, both parent-to-child and sibling incest. Reports of mother-son incest are rare,

1. *The Ladies' Home Journal*, November 1984.

accounting for fewer than 5 percent of all clinical cases. Father-daughter incest is much more prevalent, with father-son incest following behind. Daughters are twice as likely as sons to be victims overall. Although it is difficult to get a clear picture of the incidence of sibling (brother-sister) incest, clinical experience with families and adult survivors suggests that it is quite common.

Incest usually comes to light during psychiatric investigations of other seemingly unrelated symptoms (e.g., running away, severe truancy, adolescent promiscuity, unexplained vomiting, or overstimulated play in younger children). Children who are untreated victims of incest who arrive at camp with their secret may appear especially provocative, distrustful, or anxious. Adolescents may be distrustful, lethargic, or depressed or may run away as their time at camp draws to a close. It is important to remember, however, that the symptoms of incest in a child are also the symptoms evidenced by children in different circumstances. Professional training is usually needed to spot the existence of incest, and even professionals can miss the signs. If in doubt, consult a trusted professional such as a pediatrician or child therapist.

Sexual Abuse or Child Molestation

Sexual abuse is most often perpetrated by someone the child knows well—someone the child admires and reveres, who is skilled at enlisting the child's trust and confidence.

Over 90 percent of child molesters are male. The victims fall into two major categories, including prepubescent boys, ages seven to twelve, and junior-high-school-aged girls twelve to fourteen years old. (While there are certainly incidents of sexual abuse among nursery-school-aged children and younger, the emotional shock of such reports may make them seem more prevalent than they actually are.) Child molesters are usually quite comfortable with and intuitively knowledgeable about children. This makes it especially important to know more about child molesters' characteristics so we know what to look for when screening staff.

Physical Abuse

Physical abuse, also known by mental health professionals as battered child syndrome, is probably the most problematic area of child abuse for camp directors because it is more prevalent than sexual abuse and harder to define. Most clinicians can establish the presence of a physically abusive situation only if there is a repeated pattern of physical assaults or if an isolated incident is especially severe. Most physical abuse is perpetrated by parents who feel overwhelmed with parenting tasks and have little or no support or relief from their own problems or stress. It is important to remember that any situation with enough stress, in combination with little support or guidance, can result in physical abuse of children even from the most unlikely candidates.

Neglect and Emotional Abuse

Neglect and emotional abuse—probably the most common form of abuse, either at home or in any child-care agency—is also the most difficult to document. In camping, where the quality of the counselor-camper relationship is vital to the success of the season for all parties concerned, it is important to be aware of conditions that increase the chances for neglect or emotional abuse.

How to Screen for Child Abusers

There has been some talk about screening for child abuse among staff by using criminal checks, reference checks, and questions on applications and in interviews concerning prior convictions. While these are important avenues to be considered, many directors are also looking for more subtle, yet effective, approaches to the problem—approaches they can feel comfortable with themselves, knowing that they involve less of a chance of offending candidates, while still being serious about the issue. The key lies in knowing what characteristics to look for in candidates that would mitigate against hiring them—elements that can be gleaned in less awkward and offensive ways from an interview. To make sense of these characteristics, we need to look at both the profile of an abuser and the interview process itself.

When talking about abusers, we must distinguish between a person who is apt to physically abuse a child and a potential child molester, since the profiles of each are slightly different. Knowing the profile of a child molester is especially important because the characteristics of a potential or habitual child molester may, at first glance, be exactly the kind of things you look for in a good counselor. This is where fine-tuning your interview will be important.

People who are prone to physical abuse of children—that is, of dealing with children in ways that may lead to an abusive incident or pattern—tend to have been physically abused as children themselves. Severe corporal punishment can often be found in the history of physical abusers who then seem to make unrealistic demands both on themselves (trying to do too much or being perfectionistic, for example) and on children. They often exhibit a curious sense of rightness, expressing attitudes like, "If you give in to kids, they'll be spoiled," and they are overly concerned about "teaching kids to obey authority." This type of person also has a difficult time asking for help with his or her own problems and is apt to be less of a team player when it comes to working in concert with other adults. Such people will often dismiss the need to plan for dealing with stress or deny that it is a problem. They may also have trouble establishing emotional support for themselves among peers. Instead, they are prone to use their time with children to fulfill their own needs or to validate their sense of competence or well-being. What is confusing about potential physical abusers is that they often have a genuine desire to do something good for children, yet may handle them in harsh or authoritarian ways with little sense of a child's true feelings or needs.

Child molesters, by contrast, are much more tuned in to children's needs and are, in fact, highly skilled at engendering the trust and confidence of children. They are often very sensitive to children's feelings and weaknesses and have a facility for putting children, especially fearful or uncertain children, at ease. Over 80 percent of all child molesters were themselves molested as children, and, for various reasons, these individuals have extreme difficulty developing satisfying, supportive, or intimate relations with other adults. Many child molesters are drifters or loners who may have an employment history with difficult-to-explain gaps or sudden or frequent job changes. They have few friends or, for that matter, no significant other adults in their lives, with a tremendous imbalance between time spent with children and time spent with adults or peers. Such people often cite relaxing or productive times with children as their idea of time off.

After considering the profile of a child abuser, we must then screen for these characteristics in the context of a general interview. Looking for warning signs is not the only order of business, however. A good interview is really an exchange of information—a mutual sizing up—where your potential staff is given as clear an idea as possible about the demands of the job, including the hazards of burnout, as well as what it is like to work with you during the summer, how available you and other senior staff will be, and what your ground rules are, including grounds for dismissal. When screening for potential child abusers is done in the company of these other goals, it yields more information without interjecting unnecessary awkwardness or hostility between you and the candidate. Let's look then at some general aspects of interviewing that can help get the job done with greater ease and accuracy.

One of the problems with interviews for camp is that your different staff members may conduct different kinds of interviews. Consequently, their impressions of applicants may be very subjective and inconsistent. It is important to gather together all staff who conduct interviews and standardize their approaches. Develop a form that gives everyone a similar format and frame of reference, and practice on each other. Some of the tips that follow might be useful while developing your own strategies.

A second problem with interviews is that many people who conduct them make their decisions based on some intuitive sense of the candidate, known as getting a good feel for the person. While this approach may work well most of the time, you are probably applying some kind of system you've developed over the years that has carried you so far. You may be taking a sizable risk by continuing to do so. Remember that people who molest children are often quite likable, are very good with children, and sell themselves well. While there is no guaranteed method of screening out molesters and abusers, a more methodical, scientific

156

approach to interviewing can significantly reduce the percentage of risk. And while the truth is that you will still ultimately make your choice based upon some kind of intuitive feel, you will have made it a more informed decision—and, if you document, date, and sign your interview form, this can help protect you should you ever end up in court.

Another aspect of interviewing has to do with anxiety—yours and that of the interviewee. Most interviewers try to dissipate anxiety much too quickly by being extremely friendly and welcoming and by closing the distance between themselves and the person across from them. However, anxiety is a useful tool. If you put the candidate at ease too quickly, you may miss the opportunity to pick up information that can otherwise be hidden or shielded from you—something the candidate may not even be aware he or she is doing. Remember, getting a sense of how someone reacts under stress is an important thing to know. Be cordial and businesslike in the beginning. There will be plenty of time to warm up and be friendly and accepting later in the interview. Besides, taking the job seriously is a good message to send prospective counselors. Add the fun later.

Get Personal

Working in a camp setting means working with a variety of people in close quarters. Because of this, it is important to get some sense about the personal history and qualities of an individual.

There are two important considerations to take into account when asking personal questions of a candidate, the first of which is timing. An interview is really an unfolding of layers of closeness, with the more superficial, less threatening questions coming first so there is an opportunity for you and the other person to form a connection. More personal questions come further into the interview, once you have established a dialogue. I usually wait twenty minutes or so into an hour-long interview before I move in with the more personal questions.

Once you are ready to ask questions of a more personal nature, it is then important to prepare the candidate by prefacing your remarks with an explanation of your motives, giving them an opportunity to pass on answering certain questions and offering reassurance about confidentiality. The words I use are something like the following:

> Since camping is a business that's involved with people, I am interested in getting some idea about how you are with people and what your own personal background is like. I'd like to ask you some personal questions. Your answers, of course, will be confidential. Just answer whatever you feel comfortable with.

Once you have laid the groundwork, go ahead with your questions. These are the kinds of questions I include in this part of the interview.

> Do you have a best friend? Tell me about him or her: How long have you known your friend? What's one thing your friend has taught you or done for you?

Would you say you are most comfortable with people your own age, older, or younger? (Explore this.)

What kind of punishment or discipline do you think works best with children?

Proceed with some details about the job and its demands, giving some details about the more stressful aspects. Then ask such questions as: "What will you do to handle this kind of stress?" "What specific things do you think would be a problem for you?" "What would you do with your time off?" Notice how realistic the answers are regarding managing stress or maintaining a balance between work and play, along with the exposure to children and peers. The truth is that even well-meaning counselors who have many internal strengths and no prior history of physical abuse can become susceptible to it if they don't recognize and plan for the demands of camp life.

One last rich source of useful information concerns the use of hypothetical situations, preferably true-to-life examples, from previous seasons at camp that required an intervention from staff with a camper or group of campers. When asking such questions, be careful to explain at the outset that you understand that different people approach problems differently and that there are no right or wrong answers. Then be careful not to nod approval or disapproval or give other nonverbal signals as the person responds. Look for things such as asking other staff for help or support; knowing the importance of utilizing a relationship with the child; resorting to punitive measures (how quickly); giving realistic or honest responses; using games or activities to diffuse tense situations. Remember that, although this can be an anxiety-laden part of the interview, it can give you information that is very revealing and can be useful for clueing candidates into some of the realities of the job.

Red Flags

So now that you've completed the interview, how do you assess the information? Let's look at what I call "red flags"—warning signs that need careful consideration.

First of all, who is running the interview, you or the candidate? If you find yourself being on the defensive, answering a lot of questions yourself, or being distracted by tangential conversation, slow down and get back on track. If the trend persists throughout the interview, raise a red flag. Such behavior should make you wonder just what it is that a person might be avoiding.

One of the single most important things to look for in all prospective staff members is how much of a peer support system they have. Are they drifters? Are there other significant adults in their lives currently? Are there best friends or strong connections to others besides children to give you the sense of there being some balance and support in their lives? If you get a lot of negative responses, start raising the red flags.

Another factor related to adult support includes things like whether the prospective candidates are team players. Do they spend too much free time with children? Do they either dismiss the importance of free time or have difficulty telling you exactly what it is they do to rejuvenate themselves? If they have an unrealistic perception of the demands of the job that persists after you've outlined them and seem to plan time-off activities that either sound like too much work to you (typical of a physical abuser) or involve more time with children, then raise another red flag. In fact, the most serious cause for a red-flag alert is the feeling that a person spends too much time with children and has weak peer relationships.

When considering impressions from an interview, remember that the overall picture is what is important. Each person you see may have one or two areas that, because of personality or age, may raise a red flag or two. Keeping your perspective and watching for overall patterns is more important than one or two isolated items out of place. If you are undecided, review your results and impressions with a colleague.

Good interviewing techniques, like any other highly developed skill, take practice. Considering the fact that your staff may be the single most important factor in the success of your season (and in the ongoing reputation of your camp), the effort you put into it will more than pay for itself.

159

General Questions Regarding Child Abuse

1. Better reporting and more awareness has resulted in an increase in reported child abuse.
2. Programs to increase awareness in children have resulted in some false accusations.
3. What was once written off as toughening process, especially for boys, is no longer acceptable.
4. Child's sense of safety must be respected.
5. Counselor who is contrite should be helped, not punished—may not have understood actions constituted abuse.

Many camp directors have written or called me over the past several months with questions about child abuse. One recurring question is echoed by a couple in the Southwest who ask, "Bob, is there really more child abuse occurring, or is this merely the media exploiting an emotionally charged issue?"

Another camp director from the Northeast called with a situation in which a nineteen-year-old male counselor was involved in some horseplay with a group of nine-year-old boys. When the counselor "grabbed at" the genitals of several of the boys, two of the boys felt violated and later reported the incident to their parents. These parents, in turn, complained to the director that they should have been told about the incident and that the counselor should have been dismissed.

"Bob," the director lamented, "my counselor certainly exercised poor judgment, but is this truly abuse? And isn't some of this mild hazing activity just a case of boys being boys?"

While the issue of child abuse has stirred a range of responses from fear and hysteria to denial, there is some useful, sensible information available to directors that can serve both to minimize parental concerns and to ensure a safer environment for campers. Let me start with the question from the Southwest.

Between 1974 and 1986, there was an 856-percent increase in the number of child abuse cases reported in this country.[1] The key here, however, is the word "reported." Prior to 1974, many states had inad-

1. National Center for Missing and Exploited Children, Washington, D.C.

equate reporting procedures, no reporting mandates or guidelines, and, in some cases, no agency designated to process such complaints.

Currently members of the allied mental health field believe that the number of abuse cases has not increased, but rather the awareness of signs of abuse and the mechanisms for dealing with abuse situations have been better developed. Indeed, in 1984 the National Committee for Prevention of Child Abuse set as one of its long-range goals a commitment to reducing child abuse in the United States by 20–25 percent. To that end, a massive educational and public relations campaign was launched, designed to make parents, teachers, and child-care workers, as well as children themselves, more aware of child abuse.

As with any well-intentioned program, there are often negative side effects. One of these has been the increase in false accusations by children against adults—in camp, against counselors. Whereas prior to 1984 it was held that children rarely made up stories about being abused, today it is often the case that children do this.

But what of the boys-will-be-boys syndrome referred to by the director in the Northeast? First of all, what was once accepted by most children with a kind of grin-and-bear-it attitude in the past as part of the rites of passage at school or camp is now tolerated less and less. This change is part of the evolution of empathy and awareness by children and adults alike, of creating an "envelope of safety" for children in places where we want them to thrive. What was once considered a toughening process, especially for boys, is now seen as a lack of respect for personal boundaries and emotional safety.

If a child's sense of safety is not respected, then poor judgment becomes abuse. For example, holding children down and tickling them to the point where they lose bladder control or feel powerless (thus, victimized) meets the criteria of abuse. Inflicting a sense of helplessness on children, even under the ruse of a game, is, in fact, abusive and results in a repeating cycle of abuse. For example, we now know from treating child molesters that abuse begets abuse—up to 90 percent of all child molesters were sexually abused when they were children.

The key to a director's response, however, whether to the child, the offending counselor, or parents, is a measured reaction without hysteria based on an understanding of the needs of each party. Children have a right to thrive in an emotionally safe environment and have become more vocal in demanding just that.

The counselor who is embarrassed when confronted by his actions and who is genuinely contrite is entitled to better training, guidelines, and supervision. It may never have occurred to the counselor from the Northeast that he was being abusive. In fact, the issue is not whether he is a child molester, but whether he violated a child's sense of personal well-being. Furthermore, a counselor cannot teach what he hasn't learned or "be" with children in a way he hasn't experienced himself. If part of his childhood legacy is having been hazed by his caretakers, he is at risk for passing on the same behavior unless helped to know why he should do otherwise. He should be helped rather than punished.

Likewise, parents need to know that their children's need for trust and emotional safety will be taken seriously (which is not the same as a guarantee that their children will be fully protected from every possible harm). A director who minimizes parents' concerns for their child or who dismisses a problem as an overreaction by the child to horseplay is inviting a more serious challenge from parents, including a possible lawsuit.

Guidelines for Training Staff about Child Abuse

---

1. Timing—later in orientation.
2. Tone—concern for staff's well-being, not accusatory.
3. Be direct.
4. Keep it simple—don't lose their attention.
5. Be specific—give clear guidelines. Talk about:
   - hazing
   - showers, changing, undressing, sharing beds
   - touch
   - adolescent girls' crushes on male staff
   - stress
   - staff being accused

Dear Bob,

With a lot of attention being given these days to child abuse, I wonder if you have some specific ideas about how to approach the topic with staff. We have had concerns about unnecessarily upsetting some staff members or leaving our staff with the impression that we don't trust them. What are some practical guidelines?

California Calling

Dear California,

163

Thank you for your direct inquiry about staff training regarding child abuse. Many directors do not include this topic as a regular part of orientation. Some fear they may alienate their staff; others feel the chance of an actual incident at their camp is quite remote; still others believe, in an almost superstitious way, that if you don't talk about a problem, it will go away by itself. None of these assumptions is true, and it has become clear that staff people want clear guidelines in order to act appropriately with children. Here are some tips I suggest.

Use good timing. Discussions about child abuse should come later in the orientation schedule, after staff members have been given ample opportunity to build a sense of trust, cooperation, and team spirit. Scheduling a talk on child abuse too soon in the program will come across as abrupt and awkward. Staff members are your number one resource. They need time (and facilitated exercises) to open up and develop as a team.

Watch your tone. The most effective way to introduce the issue of child abuse is to express it in terms of a general concern for the well-being of the staff. Here are some words I use:

> There has been a lot of news in the last few years about a subject that probably makes most of us uneasy, but of which we need to be aware for our own well-being. I am talking about child abuse. In fact, there has been so much exposure in the media that many children have become hyper-sensitive to it, and many will misconstrue something you do as abusive unless you are clear and careful about your actions with them. I want all of you to take care of yourselves this summer, and part of taking care of yourself is being sensitive to a child's sense of emotional and physical safety. The last thing any of you need is to be accused of abusing a child who has become frightened and who has misinterpreted something you've done.

Notice that I give everyone the benefit of the doubt at this point, a tactic crucial to maintaining the sense of high positive regard for your staff that you have been working on throughout orientation.

Be direct. Being vague about the subject matter (which, by the way, should include physical and sexual as well as emotional abuse) is the worst thing you can do. Counselors should be given particular examples in clear language. If you are not comfortable talking about the topic, find someone on your key staff who is, or get a *trusted* outside expert (the camp physician, for instance) to come in for an hour to speak on the subject.

Keep it simple. You don't need to anticipate every possible situation or answer every conceivable question. If your anxiety causes you to get long-winded or convoluted, you will lose your staff's attention when you need it most. (By the way, a staff member who continues to press you with hypothetical questions about potential abuse when everyone else has tuned out is trying to tell you something about his or her anxiety or issues. This is not cause for alarm, but it is an invitation for discreet, supportive supervision.)

Be specific. The best way to keep it simple is to give clear, specific guidelines. Here are my suggestions.

1. *Talk about hazing.* You may never have had it at your camp, but new staff members bring their own experiences. Ask the staff to share them; then be clear—in a nonjudgmental, but firm, way—about what is and what is not acceptable at your camp.
2. *Talk openly about showers, changing clothes, and undressing.* I strongly suggest that no counselor be alone with one camper in any of these situations. This protects campers from the would-be abuser who may have slipped through your screening and protects the counselors from false accusations.
3. *Talk about sharing beds.* It is asking for trouble to have a camper—even a young, upset one—share a bed or sleeping bag

with a counselor (even a married one). Children who are half asleep can become confused about reality.

4. *Talk about touch.* You do not want to discourage affection (although at least one camp I know of has), but touching needs to be done in the presence of other adults. Also, I limit clingers for the sake of the development of their own independence as well as to minimize confusion. Furthermore, a child who recoils at even a simple touch (perhaps a hand on a shoulder) needs to have his boundaries respected. Back rubs and such should be done with other people around, with time limits, with clothes on, and never on a counselor's bed.

5. *Talk about adolescent crushes.* Male staff members working with adolescent females should know that girls fantasize elaborate romantic relationships that often have little or no basis in reality (a kind of practice behavior that can become quite intense). Overstimulating a teenage girl's imagination by singling her out for long private talks and encouraging a lot of one-on-one time with her without other people around has gotten at least three male staff members at different camps into trouble in the last three years—trouble that was innocent, yet avoidable.

6. *Talk about stress.* Stress is a normal part of a camp and can cause even a well-seasoned counselor to emit a "killer" state-ment to a camper. Have your staff identify sources of their stress (as well as sources of camper stress), and then brain-storm ways to manage it (since it will never go away, and it is not all bad).

7. *Talk about accusations.* Go one step further and talk about the possibility of a counselor being accused of abuse by a camper during the season. Inform your staff that, should this occur, you will ask the counselor to remove him- or herself from the campers until the accusation can be investigated. It is impor-tant that your staff understand that making this request does not mean you have decided he or she is guilty. It means that you are protecting the staff member as well as the camper until you can do a more thorough investigation.

This kind of frank, direct, practical talk about child abuse can be quite powerful, especially when it is realistic about the stress, responsi-bility, and required care of the job. I have seen it actually enhance the alliance with staff, since you as director can frame it as concern for their basic well-being.

When Campers Disclose Sexual or Physical Abuse

1. Kids often use camp as a forum to tell about abuse because they feel safe there.
2. Since girls are abused mostly by a family member, they're ten times more likely to disclose at camp.
3. Since boys are more often abused outside the family, camp is more frequently the scene of abuse for them and less frequently a place to disclose.
4. Disclosure to counselors puts them in an awkward position. Steps for counselors to take:
   - go directly to director (discloser's right to privacy) and do not tell other staff
   - director's role:
     damage control
     staff need emotional support, too.
     must report to state by law (get to know someone at the state reporting agency)
     report in state where abuse occurred
     use ACA hotline

Dear Bob,

At our camp for girls this last summer, we experienced a problem we have never had to deal with before. One of our campers told a friend—another camper—that she had been sexually abused by a friend of the family. This information was not only upsetting to the girls in the cabin, but also greatly upsetting to the staff members who became aware of it. In addition, we were not sure what to do with this information. Obviously we were concerned about this child's welfare, but it was not clear to us what to say to her, what to say to her parents, or even what our legal responsibilities were. Can you shed some light on this difficult topic?

Distraught in Pennsylvania

Dear Distraught,

The incident you describe—a camper revealing that he or she is being or has been sexually or physically abused—is referred to as *disclosure*. From an informal survey of camps across the United States, disclosure at camp seems to be on the rise.

This is not surprising when one considers that children do not make a disclosure unless they feel safe in their environment. Given that most camps work very hard to create such an atmosphere, it is not uncommon for children to use the opportunity to make their emotionally devastating secret known.

Girls tend to make disclosures at camp ten times more frequently than boys. One reason for this is that girls are more typically sexually abused inside the family—by an uncle, cousin, father, stepfather, mother's boyfriend, or brother—than are boys. (Boys are sexually abused outside the family eleven times more frequently than girls. This puts a boy more at risk in a place like camp, for example, than it does a girl.)

Since the scene of the crime for most girls is within their families, being at camp means a temporary respite from the abuse. As a girl begins to feel increasingly safe at camp (or as she comes closer and closer to going back to the source of the abuse), she may take a chance and make her disclosure. Since boys are most likely to be victimized *outside* the family, camp may not be perceived by them as being as safe a place to take a stand as it is for girls—boys may associate camp with another time when they were made to "feel funny." This may have nothing to do with camp itself; it is simply the association a boy may make to feeling unsafe outside his family.

Another reason boys are much less likely to make a disclosure at camp has to do with gender-related shame. Because 90 percent of the offenders who perpetrate sexual abuse against boys are heterosexual males, many boys become confused about what it means that a man touched them in some way. They often conclude that there is something gravely wrong with them *as males*. Since girls are also most typically abused by heterosexual males, the confusion that comes from a same-gender experience is not present. As devastating as *any* abuse experience is, the added burden of questioning one's womanhood is not at stake for most girls.

The way most girls reveal their secret is much the way you have described in your letter. First, a camper swears a friend to secrecy and discloses the information to her. That camper, upset by the news, goes to a trusted counselor and, after demanding that she promise never to tell anyone, passes along the secret.

That counselor is now in a terrible double bind. Does she go to the director and get help, thereby losing the trust of her confidante, or does she remain loyal to the camper, only to live with the knowledge that a young girl is allegedly at risk with no chance of rescue?

Counselors need support around this issue. During orientation they need to be told that disclosure by campers is a real possibility. They should be instructed to tell the child, whether the actual victim or the informant friend, the following:

1. "I am glad you told me."
2. "Having a secret like this all alone must be terrible."
3. "I believe you" (even if you do not know whether what the girl is saying is true).

4. "What kind of a friend would I (we) be if I (we) did not get you (your friend) the help you (she) need(s)?"
5. "I think the reason you told me (she told you) in the first place is because you want (she wants) some help."
6. "You have (your friend has) a right to be safe and get help."
7. "There is a difference between *confidence* and keeping secrets. Keeping secrets can hurt people; confidence keeps people's feelings *from* being hurt."
8. "There are people whose job it is to help children exactly like you (your friend)."

Some other pointers:

- Counselors must agree to go directly to camp administrators and that they will not tell other staff. Children have a right to their privacy. They worry about who knows.
- Don't expect staff to remember what you may have covered during orientation. If they encounter a camper who makes a disclosure to them, you will have to coach them through the process.
- Find out who else knows. Damage control is crucial to the well-being of the child and the other campers and staff. You need to ask your staff to rise above gossip.
- Staff will need their own emotional support. As you enlarge the envelope of confidentiality, you might include trusted staff—the camp nurse or doctor or a trusted consultant. You may want to give staff things to read, such as excerpts from this book. Remember, there may be someone on your staff who has had an experience similar to that of the child making the disclosure. That staff person may need extra support.
- Your legal responsibility is bound by state law. All states now have a fairly uniform mandated reporting law. This states that anyone in a caretaking role with children (including counselors) are mandated to report *suspected abuse*. It is not your job, nor the job of your staff, to verify the allegation or disclosure. Find out what the law is in your state.
- Reports are actually made in the state in which the abuse allegedly took/is taking place. If your camper is from out of state, get your state reporting agency to help you make the proper contacts.
- Be sure to acquaint yourself with a representative of your reporting agency *before* you actually need them. Many directors invite an agency representative into camp during orientation to talk with staff about child abuse and reporting laws. Having a preexisting relationship with an agency comes in handy if you need it during a crisis.

- Another resource for help in reporting child abuse is the National Child Abuse Hotline (800-422-4453).
- Consider using the ACA hotline (317-342-8456 during regular business hours; 317-831-8190 during evenings and weekends). While the ACA does not dispense legal or medical advice, it can help you sort through the questions and explore options and resources. It has helped many directors in times of need.

Overexposure: An Unwanted Incident at Camp

1. If an inadvertent incident threatens trust with parents, the parents must be told about it.
2. Tell campers you're going to inform parents before you call.
3. Campers may react with fear or guilt
   - they may have been titillated by incident and won't want parents to know that
   - they'll worry they're getting counselor in trouble (campers may believe they, rather than the counselor, are guilty)
   - they need relief from fear and guilt—they need you to tell parents but will beg you not to
4. Promise you will speak up with the parents if they overreact.

Dear Bob,

An incident occurred at our residential camp this summer while a group of fourteen-year-old female campers were on a sailing trip. We heard through the grapevine that the twenty-year-old male staff member from another camp who was skipper of the boat exposed himself to the girls.

The incident turned out to be less serious than we had originally thought, so we were of two minds when it came to deciding what, if anything, to say to the parents of the campers. On the one hand, we didn't want to create a problem where there wasn't one; yet, we felt we had some responsibility to the parents.

What would your advice have been?

Wondering in Wisconsin

Dear Wondering,

Many camp directors wrestle with what to tell parents and what to leave alone. The concern, generally, is how to keep from inciting unwarranted reactions from parents that might be detrimental to the child, the camp, or both. My rule of thumb is: don't create a problem when there isn't one; but don't avoid one if it comes up.

In your case, the problem already exists. What you describe is clearly a charged situation for your campers, and, whenever something overstimulating happens to campers, at least one out of the group will relate the incident to a parent during the postseason. Ask yourself whether you would rather have the parent find out about such an incident by chance after the summer or directly from you in a manner that demonstrates that you are on top of the situation. I suspect if parents were to find out after the fact and not from you, they'd feel as if they'd been deceived and would therefore be angry about a violated trust. What might have been a minor incident then becomes inflamed by the issue of trust.

I have discovered that clear, direct communication with parents in such potentially provocative situations actually enhances your alliance with them. You are telling them you are tuned into their child's well-being, respectful of their concern as parents, and unafraid to bring up delicate situations when it is necessary. This kind of direct approach puts you in a position of strength and is refreshing to most parents.

Now that I have addressed your questions, I want to discuss another aspect of the situation that has to do with the campers and what their reactions would have been had you told them of your intentions to inform their parents. Let me proceed as if it were still summer and you had just found out about the incident.

Unless you want to risk losing all trust with the campers, you must inform them of your intent to tell their parents before you actually call. You can anticipate at least two reactions: guilt and fear.

Since the experience was of a somewhat forbidden (and I assume, from what you say, not dangerous) nature, the girls will want to hide the fact that it was also somewhat stimulating. That is the last thing they will want their parents to know. Their secret fear is that parents might find out that they were titillated by something forbidden, which, by the way, is why we find out about such things through the grapevine rather than directly. These campers feel guilty about hiding the truth and probably also feel worried that they might be getting this "poor" counselor in trouble. In their minds they, not the counselor, were the guilty parties, since a part of them was excited by the forbidden nature of what he did.

I am dissecting all of this because there are lessons in it. First, the girls need relief from fear and guilt, which means they *need* you to tell their parents, but they will beg you not to. Second, everything that I have described here is intuitive, so you need to be wise about how you proceed and not sound accusatory, moralizing, or glib.

Here's what you should say to the girls.

1. "We're glad you told us. Talking about these things can be embarrassing, and you know how adults can be sometimes." You're insinuating that adults can sometimes overreact, but that you won't.
2. "We can understand why you didn't come to us right away. You were probably worried about what we'd do or what we'd say." This relieves guilt and establishes trust.
3. "Even though what the counselor did may seem minor, he was wrong to do it. What happened was his responsibility and he knows better." This sets the record straight on their not being

the guilty ones. After some discussion, proceed with your next move.

4. Be direct about the fact that, even through they, as campers, might not like the idea, you, as the director, must tell their parents what happened. (Be ready for Mt. St. Helen's to erupt!)
5. Acknowledge how they feel, showing that you fully understand why they feel the way they do.
6. Explain that they have done nothing wrong that needs to be hidden from their parents. Remind them that it was the counselor who was wrong, not them. You might also educate them about parents, saying that, if their parents aren't told and find out later, they will be angry, and justifiably so.
7. Most important, assure them that you will not abandon them by allowing their parents to misunderstand, overreact, accuse them, or take them out of camp; that you will go to bat for them with their parents, if necessary, although you don't think it will come to that.

At this point, some of the campers will say such things as, "You don't know my father!" To this you reply that you won't let their parents' irrationality get the best of the situation.

You are telling these young women that it's possible to be overrun with fears, doubts, indecision, and uncertainty and yet not be ruled by them. It is the kind of stance that will strengthen your alliance with parents and campers alike, and it is an essential lesson—you can be proud they learned it at camp.

172

child abuse and other sensitive issues

Guidelines for Camper-Counselor Contact[1]

Name _____ Camp _____

Guidelines for the Discipline of Children

I understand and accept the following:

1. Counselors may, under no circumstances, hit a child.
2. Counselors may not use abusive or derogatory language with campers.
3. Counselors need to ask for help.
4. A staff member who encounters a particularly difficult child will seek the assistance of supervisory or administrative staff.
5. In all dealings with campers, counselors should strive to *respond* as opposed to *react* to children.

Guidelines for Camper-Counselor Contact

I understand and accept that, when touching campers, the following guidelines should be followed:

- on the hand, shoulder, or upper back
- never against a child's will (unless in the case of clear and present danger to the child)
- never against a child's discomfort, whether expressed verbally or nonverbally
- in the company of other adults
- never when it would have the effect of **overstimulating** a child
- never in a place on a child's body that is normally covered by a bathing suit, unless for a clear medical necessity, and then *only with supervision by another adult*

Counselor Responsibility

I understand and accept that I am a **caretaker of children**.

I understand that there is a clear **power difference** between myself and campers (money, mobility, authority, experience, knowledge, different set of rules).

I understand that inappropriate sexual contact with or physical abuse of a camper can have severe emotional and psychological effects on that camper that can last a lifetime. These reactions can be so severe, they can require intensive professional intervention which can be disruptive to the victim's life as well as time consuming and expensive.

1. Copyright 1994, little fox productions, ltd. Used with permission of the publisher.

State Laws Pertaining to Child Abuse

I am aware of the following:

definition of "mandated reporter"

purpose of law

clarification that a report is based on suspicion of abuse, not proven abuse

summary of procedure (time frame, reporting agency, information requested)

penalty for not reporting

Guidelines for Staff

I understand and accept the following:

- There is no "hazing" of campers by campers or counselors.
- Campers will not be subjected to "initiation" rites that are abusive in any manner.
- There will be double coverage of campers by adults during changing times.
- Younger children should be encouraged to change their own clothes as much as possible.
- Campers will not be alone with a counselor in his or her quarters.
- A staff member will under no circumstance share a bed or sleeping bag with a camper.
- Counselors will set limits with children who "cling" or hang on them.
- Counselors will not give back rubs unless another adult is present, and then only with clothes on.
- Tickling or teasing a camper to the point where that camper is out of control is unacceptable.
- Pillow fights or wrestling matches and the like can become overstimulating in short order and need to be limited and carefully supervised.
- Overnights need a minimum of two adult leaders. There needs to be at least one counselor present of the same gender as the campers.
- Counselors sleeping together on overnights is grounds for dismissal.
- Romantic lives of counselors can, under no circumstance, be shared with campers.
- Counselors should stay out of cabins after lights out at night unless on specific camp business.

174

- Male staff working with adolescent females need to be aware of the tendency for this group to develop hidden or secret romantic fantasies.
- *Whatever is done with campers should be done in broad daylight—with company!*

Other Instructions
I agree to the following:

- to watch for signs of stress in myself and others as a way of maintaining a safe environment at camp
- to help other staff who seem at risk for hurting or abusing campers
- to alert senior or supervisory personnel to dangerous or "at-risk" situations between campers and staff
- to ask for more supervision, intervention, or support
- to seek help myself if I feel at risk for hurting, overstimulating, or abusing a camper

By signing this document I am attesting to the fact that I have seen the videotape entitled, "Maintaining an Envelope of Safety—Guidelines for Camper-Counselor Contact."

Furthermore, I am attesting, by signing below under penalty of perjury, to the fact that I have read, understand, and accept the rules, guidelines, and standards of conduct outlined in this document.

175

_____   _____
(signed)   (witness)

_____
(date)

Professional Readings — Reading as Professionals

One of the keys to developing a more effective partnership with parents is becoming a source of information and knowledge about children and children's issues. While parents should not expect camping professionals to have the level of knowledge that pediatricians, psychiatrists, psychologists, or other child experts have attained, they should be able to count on directors having some awareness of current and emerging issues in the field of child development, health, and education. It means that anyone working with children must be concerned about his or her own professional development. It means that camping professionals need to be readers.

Whenever someone enters the field of medicine, mental health, education, or recreation, she or he is expected to catch up on the knowledge base that forms the foundation of thinking and practice in that discipline. Camping professionals are no exception. Indeed, given that camping folks see a broad spectrum of issues and concerns in the children of families they serve, it makes sense that they should be reading a range of material. What follows is a short list of what I consider essential reading for any professional working with children.

Rather than philosophical or theoretical, most of these selections are loaded with information, professional observations, and practical advice. The Selma Fraiberg classic, *The Magic Years*, first published in 1959, is still one of the best discussions of early childhood one can read. Folks wishing to speak with more authority about the challenges of parenting children and raising families in the 1990s should gobble up Anthony Wolf's *It's Not Fair. . .!* and Mary Pipher's *The Shelter of Each Other*. Other selections cover attention deficit disorder, eating disorders, current issues regarding girls, notions for working with and surviving teens, and the most relevant selections for camping professionals on business and team development.

I strongly suggest that camp and day care/child care teams assign periodic reading selections and then meet at regular intervals to discuss the material. Even if the assignment is one chapter from one book, the practice provides a common base of knowledge for individuals working together. It also promotes a sense of professionalism, develops team spirit, and provides the opportunity to discuss ways of applying the information to the daily practice of the organization. Some camps and child care agencies have even developed ways to share this information with parents and other staff.

What you will not find here are selections on sexual harassment, diversity, racism, demographics, and other social issues relevant to children and families. Their absence is not a comment on my part about their value or relevance. I simply am not as qualified to give references in these areas as I am in the areas of child and teen behavior.

Bibliography

Children

Clinton, Hillary Rodham. *It Takes a Village*. New York: Simon and Schuster, 1996.
  A comprehensive look at the most recent work and research on building security, self-esteem, and competencies in children. Ms. Rodham Clinton addresses prevention, programs that inoculate children against failure, and a policy that provides for better care of all children. A must read for anyone purporting to know about children and children's issues at the turn of this century. Hardcover, 318 pp.

Coles, Robert. *The Moral Life of Children*. Boston: Houghton Mifflin, 1986.
  This is a classic piece on the moral choices children make and the focus (movies, pop culture, social class, life experience) that influences and shapes them. Coles is a prolific, clear writer who has published many other books on children's issues. Paperback, 302 pp. with index.

Faber, Adele and Elaine Mazlish. *How to Talk So Kids Will Listen & Listen So Kids Will Talk*. New York: Avon Books, 1980.
  How to listen to—and understand—a child's concerns. How to help a child attain a positive self-image. Paperback, 242 pp. with index.

Fraiberg, Selma H. *The Magic Years*. New York: Charles Scribner's Sons, 1959.
  This is a classic. Read and reread by every serious pediatrician, child psychiatrist, social worker, child therapist, teacher, and parent. Gives delightful, clear understanding of the inner world and reality of children from infancy to seven years. Essential for day camp folks, it contains knowledge all people who work with children should have: the underpinnings of most psychological and emotional issues of children of all ages. Paperback, 305 pp. with index.

Goleman, Daniel. *Emotional Intelligence*. New York: Bantam Books, 1995.
  This is a ground-breaking work that all people involved in the education or socialization of children should know about. Goleman covers the essential abilities that children develop to succeed, make friends, protect themselves, and feel good about themselves. Includes a great discussion of emotions and the brain and what opportunities and experiences enhance emotional intelligence. Hardcover, 287 pp. with appendices and index.

Kurcinka, Mary Sheedy. *Raising Your Spirited Child*. New York: Harper Collins, 1991.

> Mary Sheedy Kurcinka describes "spirited children" as those youngsters who are "intense, persistent, sensitive, perceptive and often uncomfortable with change." Written from a parent's perspective, there is much common sensible, practical information here for people who work with young children—from infancy through age 7. Explains how to anticipate troublesome events, what triggers kids, how to get through the battles and painful episodes, and more. Not only a resource for counselors and staff of younger children, but a helpful resource for the besieged parent as well. Good common sense. Paperback, 302 pp. with index.

Wolf, Anthony E. *It's Not Fair, Jeremy Spencer's parents let him stay up all night!* New York: Farrar, Straus and Giroux, 1995.

> If you have time to read only one new book on children, make it this one. A clear discussion of the competent, grown-up self versus the regressed, demanding "baby self" and how to cope. Great for staff, supervisors, parents. Paperback, 235 pp.

Specific Children's Issues

Hallowell (M.D.), Edward M. and John J. Ratey (M.D.). *Driven to Distraction*. New York: Pantheon Books, 1994.

> Recognizing and coping with Attention Deficit Disorder (ADD) from childhood through adulthood. Hardcover, 319 pp. with index.

Hancock, Emily. *The Girl Within*. New York: Fawcett Columbine, 1989.

> An interesting look back from middle age to the girl of nine or ten who was left behind. Describes the spirit, enthusiasm, and energy that were sacrificed to caretaking and how many women wish to rediscover the girl within. Hardcover, 318 pp.

Koplewicy (M.D.), Harold S. *It's Nobody's Fault*. New York: Times Books (Random House), 1996.

> A guilt-free look at understanding children with attention deficit disorder (ADD), obsessive-compulsive disorder (OCD), separation anxiety disorder, enuresis (bedwetting), Tourette syndrome, eating disorders, and others. Gives good, clear explanations of these disorders in accessible language. Resource chapter, definitions of terms, drugs, etc. Hardcover, 303 pp. with index.

Pipher, Mary. *Reviving Ophelia: Saving the Selves of Adolescent Girls*. New York: Grosset/Putnam, 1994.

> An inside look at the pressures adolescent girls experience and the inner vulnerable reality this creates for many teen girls. Paperback, 304 pp.

Pipher, Mary. *The Shelter of Each Other*. New York: G. P. Putnam's Sons, 1996.

> A refreshing, well-written, empathetic look at the plight of families today who have no spare time and tremendous commitments and who struggle to remain connected. Several case studies bring to life what Americans in the 1990s are struggling with. Includes a great chapter on what some families and communities are doing to reconnect and provide a greater safety net for the children. A must read for people working with families in the 1990s and beyond. Hardcover, 282 pp. with index.

Teens

Ponton (M.D.), Lynn. *The Romance of Risk*. New York: Harper Collins, in press (scheduled for release in 1997).

> Dr. Ponton suggests that risk-taking is an integral part of the way teens grow. In the United States she suggests risk-taking is encouraged and romanticized in our culture more than in other parts of the world. A look at positive and negative risk-taking in teens and how adults can help create more of the former and less of the latter.

Wolf, Anthony E. *Get Out of My Life! (but first could you drive me and Cheryl to the mall?)*. New York: The Noonday Press, 1991.

> The best, most down-to-earth, practical book on teens I've seen. Discusses key issues clearly; points out typical patterns for boys versus girls; provides realistic, workable strategies for curfews, confrontations, house rules, and more. A must (and fun) read for anyone working with teens. Paperback, 204 pp.

180

General Business

Covey, Stephen R. *The Seven Habits of Highly Effective People.* New York: Simon & Schuster (A Fireside Book), 1990.

> This is a landmark work, read by many camping professionals. The chapter on listening is one all key staff should read and discuss. If you want your operation to go from mediocre to outstanding—from good to great, creative and fresh—this book can serve as the springboard. Paperback, 358 pp. with index.

Senge, Peter M. *The Fifth Discipline*. New York: Bantam Doubleday Dell, 1990.

> Not for everyone—this sophisticated, somewhat academic discussion takes systems theory and applies it to the teams that operate in business settings. Probably the most valuable chapters are 10–12, which focus on teamwork, mental models, the assumptions people make that impede trust

and openness, and how personal vision and mastery can create powerful teams if harnessed properly. If you are a forward thinker, serious about helping your team become high powered learners, don't miss this book. Hardcover, 424 pp. with index.

181

Index

A

abusive behavior, 136–138
   of children, 77–79
accidental enuresis, 33
achievable goals, 9
ADD. *See* attention deficit disorder (ADD)
ADHD. *See* attention deficit hyperactive
     disorder (ADHD)
adults with ADHD, 62–63
American Camping Association (ACA), 146
   hotline, 169
anorexia nervosa, 66–67
apologies, 112–113
appropriate behavior
   counselors, 123
   enforcing, 42–43
   staff, 121–122
arguments and teens, 140
Attention Deficit Disorder: A Different
     Perception (Hartmann), 63
attention deficit disorder (ADD), 55–61
Attention Deficit Disorder in Adults (Weiss),
     63
attention deficit hyperactive disorder
     (ADHD), 6, 7. *See also* attention
     deficit disorder (ADD)
   adults with, 62–63
attention-hungry children, 9–10
audience, knowledge of, 36–37
authority issues, staff, 14–16
autonomy and boundaries in safe environ-
     ment, 3

B

bed-wetting, 33–35
binge eating disorder (BED), 66–67
bonding activities, 38–39
boys' residential camps, child abuse in, 147–
     148
brainstorming, 40–41
bulimia, 66–67
bullies, 40–41
Burns, Nancy, 25

C

Camp Director's Guide, 146
camper agreements, 44–47
camper crushes, 80–82
camper discipline, 124
camper-counselor contact, guidelines for,
     173–175
campers
   and contracting, 45–46
   growth among, 104–105
campers disclosure of child abuse, 166–169
Camping Magazine, 146

D

E

K

Kerns, Peter, 138

moderation in story-telling, 36–37
moral code, 48
moral reasoning of staff, 83–85
motivating children, 9
motor tics, 64
Moxley, Kelly Gordon, 25
music, to bring children together, 31

L

language barriers, among campers, 30–31
Lifetime and Safety Nets (Ditter), 65
limits in safe environment, 3
listening to children, 19
loss of control
   of counselors, 112–113
   fear of, 3–4

N

National Committee for Prevention of Child Abuse, 161
   hotline, 169
negative behavior, 12
negative consequences and contracting, 46
negative feedback, 100
neglect and emotional abuse, 152, 155
nocturnal enuresis, 33
nonverbal communication, 30

M

magic phrases for attention-getting, 17–18
The Magic Years (Fraiberg), 176
management by walking around (MBWA), 99
matching kids by maturity, 38–39
medication for bed-wetting, 35
Melzer, Asher, 25
mental monsters, 36

O

O'Brien, Dennis, 7, 8
observation skills for supervisors, 125
off-season contact with campers, 121–122
older staff, 111
outside speakers, 73

P

parents, 6, 130–132
    and contracting, 45
    disclosing sensitive information, 133–135
    notifying about success, 12
    notifying camp about bed-wetting, 33, 34
    panels, 73
    working with, 7
permissiveness vs. empathy, 14–15
personnel management, 119–120
physical abuse, 152, 154
Pipher, Mary, 130, 176
positive consequences, 90
    and contracting, 46
    and teens, 140
power and control stage, 19, 20
praise, 48
privacy needs of teens, 139, 140–141
professional readings, 176–177

R

readings, professional, 176–177
red flags in interviews, 158–159
redirecting behavior, 90–91
regressive pull, 72
rejection, fear of, 3
repair work for supervisors, 127
reporting child abuse, 160–162
returning staff, 111
Ritalin, 55–61
role-playing, 73
    with staff, 86–88
rule-breaking, 14–15, 42–43
rules for campers, 89–91

S

safe environment for children, 2–4
sanctioned ways of sparring, 21–22
saying goodbye, 52–53
scapegoating, 38–39
scary stories, 36–37
screening for abusers, 152, 155–157
second-year homesickness, 28–29
secret signal technique, 9, 10–11
Seinfeld, Ira, 6, 7
self-confidence, 40–41
self-control, 14–16, 77–79
    of staff, 83–85
self-esteem, 12–13
    Tourette's Syndrome and, 65
self-worth, 40–41
sensitive information, parents disclosure of, 133–135
sex and campers, 92–93, 114–116
sexual abuse, 152, 154
sexual behavior by campers, 143
The Shelter of Each Other (Pipher), 130, 176
sister program, 25–26
skills
    for counselors, 89–91
    for supervisors, 124–127
smoothing, 90
socialization of children, 131
sparring, 21–22
staff, 72–74
    appropriate behavior, 117–118, 121–122
    arguments with campers, 112–113
    as authorities on children, 83–85
    challenges, 98–101
    feedback to, 106–107
    motivation, 106–107
    opportunities for success, 109–110
    training, 86–88
strategies, 9, 10
stress in training staff about child abuse, 163, 165
success opportunities
    for children, 40–41
    for staff, 109–110
supervision of staff, 101
supervisory skills, 124–127

T

tattling, 50–51
teasing, 38–39
teens and parents, 139–142
time-outs, 48–49
timing in training staff about child abuse, 163
Tofrinil, 35
tone in training staff about child abuse, 163, 164
tools for success, 9
Tourette's Syndrome (TS), 64–65
training
    about child abuse, 163–165
    of staff, 6, 86–88
transitory regression enuresis, 33
trust
    and communication with staff, 102–103
    in safe environment, 2
tug-of-war trap, 86, 88

U

understanding issues, 9
unity building, 19–20
unwanted behavior, 48–49

V

Vinicombe, Pamela, 25
vocal tics, 64

W

Weiss, Lynn, 63
Williams, Jani Brokaw, 6, 8
Wolf, Anthony, 176
Woods, Ann, 7, 8